THE THIRD PATH

The Third Path

BEYOND WASHINGTON AND DU BOIS TOWARDS A NATION OF THINKERS, CREATORS, & ENTREPRENEURS

Anton Anthony Ed.S, ThD

Dr. Anton Anthony

Contents

1

Introduction	1
Chapter 1: Booker T. Washington:	6
Chapter 2: W.E.B. Du Bois:	15
Chapter 3: Assessing the Impact:	24
Part II: The Modern Context	32
Chapter 4: 21st Century Challenges:	33
Chapter 5: The Rise of Entrepreneurship:	43
Create Part III: The Third Path	53
Chapter 6: Redefining the Vision:	54
Chapter 7: Entrepreneurship as Empowerment:	62
Chapter 8: Removing Barriers to Entrepreneurship:	67
Chapter 9: Education for a New Era:	78
Chapter 10: Policy Proposals for a Nation of Creators	84
Conclusion: Toward a Future of Thinkers and Creators	93
Glossary	95

About The Author 99
References 101
Connect With The Author 105

Copyright © 2023 by Anton Anthony Ed.S, ThD

All rights reserved. No part of this book may be reproduced in any manner whatsoever without written permission except in the case of brief quotations embodied in critical articles and reviews.

First Printing, 2023

1

Introduction

Two figures stand out in the realm of civil rights and the empowerment of the Black community, casting long, influential shadows across the landscape of American history. Booker T. Washington and W.E.B. Du Bois, contemporaries in time but opposites in ideology, were the twin poles around which Black America oriented its struggle for progress in a society that too often denied them their rightful place. But does their influence remain relevant today, and if so, how?

Booker T. Washington, the pragmatic educator, and reformer, urged African Americans to uplift themselves through vocational skills and economic self-reliance, working within the system to gradually earn respect and acceptance. Conversely, the fiery intellectual W.E.B. Du Bois championed the cause of higher education and political activism, advocating for immediate and uncompromising equality. Their strategies were valid for their time, but do they still hold the answers for today's complex societal challenges?

As the years have passed and the struggles of the Black community have evolved, we must pose a fundamental question: were they right? Did the paths paved by Washington and Du Bois lead to the destination of social and economic equality? The answer is both yes and no.

Research shows that the COVID-19 pandemic and the rise of technology have dramatically reshaped the global economic landscape, emphasizing the need for entrepreneurship and innovation. A study by the World Economic Forum asserts that 42% of the core job skills required in 2022 were different from those needed in 2018. This rapid transformation only magnifies the limitations of Washington's and Du Bois' strategies in addressing the challenges of the 21st century.

What if the solutions proposed over a century ago, while groundbreaking for their era, did not wholly address the multifaceted challenges facing the Black community and all marginalized communities today?

This realization led to the birth of a new idea: a third path that synthesizes the most beneficial aspects of Washington's and Du Bois' philosophies while addressing their shortcomings, a path that transcends racial boundaries and speaks to the heart of human potential—Entrepreneurship.

This book, "The Third Path: Beyond Washington and Du Bois Towards a Nation of Thinkers, Creators, & Entrepreneurs," proposes that entrepreneurship and innovation—creating value from ideas—are the keys to overcoming societal and economic disparities. Why entrepreneurship, you might ask? Because it is the path that empowers every individual, regardless of their racial, ethnic, or socioeconomic background, to tap into their inherent potential to create, innovate, and make a tangible impact on their communities and the world.

Washington's wise words echo in our vision, "At the bottom of education, at the bottom of politics, even at the bottom of religion, there must be for our race economic independence." This book is a journey into redefining economic independence, not through labor but through the empowering lens of entrepreneurship.

Equally, the words of Du Bois resonate with our endeavor. He wrote in The Souls of Black Folk, "The Negro race, like all races, is going to be saved by its exceptional men." And exceptional men and women, we argue, are not just born but can be made—forged in the crucible of entrepreneurial thinking and practice.

This book serves as a manifesto for creating AA Steam & Entrepreneurship Academy—a cradle of creativity and enterprise that would nurture and guide learners to be not just workers but creators and entrepreneurs. Why an Entrepreneurship Academy? Because in a world disrupted by a global pandemic and reshaped by technology, we need more innovators who can navigate the uncertainties of the 21st century and shape the future in their unique ways.

And so, our journey begins not by discarding the past but by understanding it, appreciating it, and building upon it to forge a new path—a third path—toward a future of unbounded possibilities. Can we turn the tide? Can we redefine economic independence and catalyze a new wave of creators and entrepreneurs? With conviction, determination, and relentless pursuit of innovation, the answer is a resounding yes.

In this endeavor, we stand on the shoulders of giants—Washington and Du Bois—embracing their wisdom, acknowledging their shortcomings, and aspiring to push the envelope toward a future where everyone can unlock their entrepreneurial potential to change the world.

After all, in an increasingly complex world riddled with challenges ranging from pandemics to climate change to societal inequities, we need not merely followers of the status quo but audacious thinkers and doers. Entrepreneurs who, in their unique ways, can redefine challenges as opportunities and sow the seeds of change.

And this change begins here, with this book. A book that isn't just about understanding history or critiquing the present, but a book that seeks to shape the future—a blueprint for cultivating a generation of creators and entrepreneurs.

So, as we step forward on this journey, let's carry with us a spirit of inquiry and audacity, a passion for making a difference, and a vision to harness the power of entrepreneurship for the greater good.

Our journey is not an easy one, it will be fraught with challenges, but it's a journey that holds the promise of a better future—a future where everyone, regardless of their race, color, or socioeconomic status, can stand tall as creators, innovators, and entrepreneurs.

Through the pages of this book, we invite you to join us on this exciting expedition—a journey from the past through the present and into the future. A journey that we hope will transform not just how we view Washington and Du Bois but how we perceive the immense potential of every individual to make a difference.

Welcome to "The Third Path: Beyond Washington and Du Bois Towards a Nation of Creators & Entrepreneurs." It's time we re-imagined the world, not as it is, but as it could be—a world teeming with creators and entrepreneurs, all working together to shape a brighter, better, and more inclusive future.

Chapter 1: Booker T. Washington:

A Philosophy of Accommodation and Self-help.

Introduction

This chapter begins by examining the life and ideology of Booker T. Washington, the influential African American leader who rose from enslavement to shape the trajectory of racial progress in America post-Reconstruction era. His philosophy, marked by a strategy of accommodation and self-help, would lay the groundwork for one of the most significant debates in black social and economic progression.

Section 1: The Life and Times of Booker T. Washington

Booker Taliaferro Washington was born into slavery in 1856 on a plantation in Virginia. His early years were marked by hardship and struggle, an experience that was sadly common among enslaved African Americans. But it was from this crucible of hardship that Washington's resolve and pragmatic philosophy were forged.

After emancipation, Washington embarked on an extraordinary journey of self-education. Young Washington walked hundreds of miles to attend the Hampton Institute, one of the few educational institutions open to African Americans at the time. His tenacity and commitment to his education did not go unnoticed; his mentor at Hampton, General Samuel Armstrong, would later prove instrumental in Washington's career, assisting him in founding the Tuskegee Normal and Industrial Institute in Alabama in 1881.

Washington's years at Hampton shaped the young educator's beliefs. He saw first-hand how practical skills and self-discipline could lift his peers from poverty. This experience laid the groundwork for his philosophy of self-help and education in practical skills.

His rise to national prominence began with an address at the Cotton States and International Exposition in Atlanta in 1895, now referred to as the "Atlanta Compromise" speech. In this speech, he argued that vocational education was the key for African Americans to improve their economic status while avoiding the tensions of direct social integration.

This speech cemented Washington's status as the predominant black leader in the eyes of white America. His pragmatic approach to racial progress—focusing on economic uplift and working within the existing system—resonated with many, both blacks hoping for progress and whites eager to maintain the social order.

Throughout his life, Washington maintained a relentless commitment to his vision of racial progress through self-help and accommodation. He leveraged his national influence to secure funds and resources for Tuskegee, transforming it into a beacon of vocational education for African Americans.

His influence extended beyond education; Washington was a major advocate for black entrepreneurship. He believed that economic self-reliance was key to overcoming racial barriers. To support this belief, he established the National Negro Business League to promote the commercial and economic prosperity of African Americans.

But Washington's life and philosophy were not without controversy. His strategy of accommodation and gradualism drew criticism from other black leaders, most notably W.E.B. Du Bois, who demanded immediate social and political equality. This ideological clash would come to define the discourse of black leadership in the years to come.

Reflecting on Washington's life and times, we can see how his personal experiences with slavery, self-education, and his rise to prominence shaped his philosophy. He believed in the power of education, hard work, and economic self-reliance as the means for African Americans to carve out a place for themselves in American society. Yet, as we will explore in the next sections, this philosophy had its limitations when faced with the harsh realities of systemic racism and economic inequality.

Section 2: A Pragmatic Philosophy

Booker T. Washington's philosophy centered on the belief that African Americans could achieve social and economic equality through self-reliance, hard work, and practical education. He prioritized economic self-determination as the primary route to racial progress. This pragmatic philosophy, though controversial, was a response to the realities of post-emancipation America, marked by deep-seated racial prejudices and economic disparities.

Washington was an ardent believer in self-reliance, a value he thought indispensable for the progress of African Americans. This belief was deeply rooted in his own life experiences. Rising from the hardships of slavery and poverty, he had personally experienced how resilience and hard work could transform one's life. He believed that the same could apply to the entire African American community.

Education, particularly practical vocational education, formed the cornerstone of Washington's vision for racial progress. He held that industrial education, teaching students skills in trades and agriculture, would prepare African Americans to be self-sufficient and economically independent. In his perspective, a skilled workforce would not only elevate the individual but also the race, by creating a robust black economy.

Economic uplift, he believed, was a means of gaining respect and acceptance from whites. He reasoned that if African Americans could demonstrate their value to the economy as skilled workers and entrepreneurs, they would gradually earn the respect of their white counterparts. Washington posited that as African Americans achieved economic prosperity, their social status would naturally improve, leading to better treatment and acceptance from the white population.

Yet, a key aspect of Washington's philosophy was the idea of racial accommodation. He believed that African Americans should not agitate for immediate civil rights or social integration, but rather strive to improve their status through economic advancement. This stance was exemplified in his famous 'Atlanta Compromise' speech, where he suggested that African Americans should accept social segregation in return for economic progress.

Washington's philosophy, although pragmatic, was seen by some as a concession to the systemic racial prejudice of the time. Critics argued that his focus on economic upliftment and accommodation did not address the need for immediate civil and political rights, and therefore perpetuated racial inequalities. These critics, most notably W.E.B. Du Bois, proposed alternative strategies for racial progress, which we will explore in the next chapters.

In conclusion, Washington's pragmatic philosophy was a strategic response to the realities of his time, designed to promote self-reliance, practical education, and economic upliftment as a means for African Americans to achieve social and economic equality. However, the effectiveness and limitations of this approach become evident when examined against the backdrop of systemic racism and economic inequality that persisted during Washington's era and beyond.

Section 3: Impact and Implementation of Washington's Ideas

Booker T. Washington's impact on African American education and the broader American society can best be understood by examining the implementation of his ideas at the Tuskegee Institute and his influence on economic and educational policies.

When Washington founded the Tuskegee Normal and Industrial Institute in 1881, he envisioned a place where African Americans could acquire practical skills and work ethic, which he believed were vital to their progress. At Tuskegee, students learned various trades, such as brick masonry, carpentry, sewing, and farming, alongside traditional subjects like reading and arithmetic. Washington's educational model was focused on producing graduates who could make immediate contributions to their communities as skilled workers and entrepreneurs.

Under Washington's leadership, Tuskegee grew exponentially, both in terms of physical size and the number of students. By the early 20th century, it was one of the leading African American educational institutions in the United States. Tuskegee's success demonstrated the viability of Washington's approach to education and its ability to empower African Americans economically.

Beyond Tuskegee, Washington's philosophy greatly influenced black education throughout the South. Many schools adopted the Tuskegee model, focusing on vocational training as a means to economic independence. Washington's influence extended to white philanthropists who financed educational initiatives for African Americans. His pragmatic philosophy resonated with them, leading to significant financial support for vocational schools.

In addition to education, Washington significantly influenced African American economic development. He urged African Americans to become entrepreneurs and to create and control their own businesses. He established the National Negro Business League to support this vision, encouraging economic collaboration among African Americans.

The broader societal impact of Washington's philosophy is complex. Many African Americans, particularly those in the rural South, saw value in Washington's focus on self-help and economic advancement. His strategy offered a tangible pathway to improve their lives.

Among whites, especially in the South, Washington was widely accepted as a reasonable and safe spokesperson for African Americans. His accommodationist approach assuaged white fears about black demands for social equality and desegregation.

However, not everyone agreed with Washington's philosophy. Critics, both black and white, argued that his focus on industrial education and economic self-help, and his willingness to accommodate the racial status quo, did not challenge the systemic racism and segregation prevalent in American society. Among these critics was W.E.B. Du Bois, who offered a different perspective on how African Americans should strive for equality.

In conclusion, while Washington's philosophy had significant impact, influencing educational and economic practices for African Americans, it was not without its critics. Its true effectiveness and limitations become more apparent when juxtaposed against the contrasting ideas of his contemporaries, a discussion that will be undertaken in the following sections.

Section 4: Critiques and Limitations of Washington's Philosophy

While Booker T. Washington's philosophy of self-reliance and economic uplift had a profound impact on black America and influenced many, it was not without its critics or limitations.

Among Washington's contemporaries, perhaps the most vocal critic was W.E.B. Du Bois. Du Bois, an advocate for full civil rights and political representation for African Americans, saw Washington's approach as overly cautious and limiting. He argued that Washington's focus on vocational training neglected the need for higher education among African Americans.

Furthermore, Du Bois criticized Washington's strategy of accommodation as a concession that tacitly accepted the social and political inequality of African Americans.

Moreover, many modern critics argue that Washington's philosophy did not challenge the systemic racism that underpinned American society during his time. His belief in racial uplift through self-help and economic independence was predicated on the assumption that whites would respond positively to black progress. However, the realities of Jim Crow laws and rampant racial violence in the South demonstrated that economic success did not necessarily translate into social acceptance or civil rights.

Economic critiques also arose around Washington's philosophy. His emphasis on self-help suggested that African Americans could advance economically through individual effort, neglecting the societal and systemic barriers that hindered black economic progress. This emphasis on individual responsibility could be interpreted as ignoring or downplaying structural racism and economic inequity.

Washington's approach to education has also been scrutinized. Critics suggest that his vocational focus was too narrow and failed to equip African Americans for leadership roles in society. They argue that it was not enough to train African Americans to work within the system; they also needed to be prepared to challenge and change the system.

In light of these critiques, it's evident that while Washington's philosophy offered tangible benefits, it had significant limitations. Its focus on self-help and economic progress, although beneficial to some, was not sufficient to dismantle systemic racism or achieve full civil rights. This limitation becomes more pronounced when compared to alternative strategies, such as those proposed by W.E.B. Du Bois, a discussion that will be undertaken in the following chapter.

Chapter 2: W.E.B. Du Bois:

Advocacy for Civil Rights and the 'Talented Tenth.

This chapter examines the life, philosophy, and impact of W.E.B. Du Bois, another significant figure in African American history. A staunch advocate for civil rights and higher education, Du Bois' contributions were fundamental in shaping the struggle for racial equality in America. His perspectives offer a stark contrast to those of Booker T. Washington, presenting an alternative approach to addressing the challenges faced by African Americans during this era.

Section 1: The Life and Times of W.E.B. Du Bois

William Edward Burghardt Du Bois, better known as W.E.B. Du Bois, was born in 1868 in Great Barrington, Massachusetts. Unlike Washington, who was born into slavery, Du Bois was born free in the North and enjoyed a relatively comfortable upbringing. His early life in the mostly white town of Great Barrington would shape his views on race and equality.

His education began in the public schools of Great Barrington. Demonstrating academic prowess from an early age, Du Bois was encouraged by his teachers and supported by members of his community. His intellectual aptitude allowed him to attend Fisk University, a historically black university in Nashville, Tennessee, on a scholarship. This experience was crucial, as it exposed him to the harsh realities of racism and Jim Crow laws in the South.

After graduating from Fisk, Du Bois earned another scholarship to Harvard University, where he became the first African American to earn a Ph.D. from the institution. His time at Harvard exposed him to a wide range of political and philosophical ideas, further shaping his understanding of race relations and influencing his stance on civil rights.

Du Bois' education didn't stop at Harvard. He studied at the University of Berlin, where he was introduced to historical materialism and other theories that would significantly impact his later work. He was one of a small number of African Americans to study abroad at the time, and the experience further broadened his understanding of racial issues within a global context.

Upon returning to the United States, Du Bois embarked on a career in academia and activism. He held teaching positions at Wilberforce University and the University of Pennsylvania, and later at Atlanta University, where he conducted extensive sociological research on African American communities.

Du Bois emerged as a leading voice for civil rights, clashing with Washington's views and becoming a powerful advocate for full civil rights and political representation for African Americans. His intellectual prowess and relentless activism led to the founding of the National Association for the Advancement of Colored People (NAACP), where he served as the director of publicity and research and the editor of its magazine, The Crisis.

Throughout his life, Du Bois remained a passionate advocate for African American rights, tirelessly pushing for equality until his death in 1963. His ideas would play a major role in the civil rights movement and continue to influence discussions about race and equality to this day. Du Bois' life and career offer a contrasting perspective to Washington's, allowing us to explore an alternative approach to addressing racial inequality.

Section 2: The Philosophy of W.E.B. Du Bois

W.E.B. Du Bois was a staunch advocate for full civil rights and political representation for African Americans. His philosophy sharply contrasted with Booker T. Washington's, and their differing viewpoints represented two of the most influential schools of thought regarding racial progress in their time.

Full Civil Rights and Political Representation

Du Bois firmly believed that political action and agitation were necessary to achieve racial equality. He critiqued Washington's approach, which he felt was overly accommodating to white society's expectations and constraints. According to Du Bois, accepting discrimination and deferring civil rights aspirations would only serve to perpetuate racial inequality.

His argument for full civil rights was not merely about gaining political representation; it was also about establishing an African

American identity independent of white oppression. He fought for African Americans' rights to vote, access to quality education, and an end to segregation and discrimination.

Critique of Washington's Approach

Du Bois' critique of Washington focused on the latter's failure to challenge the systemic racism that prevailed in their time. He saw Washington's philosophy of self-help and economic progress as narrow and limited because it didn't address the structural and institutional barriers to black progress. Washington's emphasis on industrial education, according to Du Bois, overlooked the need for African Americans to pursue higher education and to aspire for leadership roles within society.

The 'Talented Tenth'

One of Du Bois' most enduring ideas was his concept of the 'Talented Tenth.' He believed that the black community's progress would be led by an educated elite who would then uplift the rest of the race. The 'Talented Tenth' referred to the top ten percent of African Americans in terms of educational attainment and intellectual capability. These individuals, according to Du Bois, would be instrumental in leading the struggle for racial equality.

Global Black Solidarity

Du Bois' philosophy extended beyond the confines of America. He was one of the early proponents of Pan-Africanism, a global intellectual movement that seeks to encourage and strengthen bonds of solidarity between all people of African descent. He organized several Pan-African conferences and consistently advocated for global black solidarity as a tool to combat colonialism and white supremacy.

Through his philosophy, Du Bois championed an alternative path to racial progress—one rooted in direct political action, higher education, and a staunch refusal to compromise on civil rights. In the next section, we'll explore how he implemented these ideas and the impact they had on American society.

Section 3: Impact and Implementation of Du Bois' Ideas

Du Bois was not just a man of ideas; he was also a man of action. He implemented his philosophy through numerous channels, including academia, activism, and organizing, which had a profound impact on African Americans and American society as a whole.

The NAACP and The Crisis

Perhaps Du Bois' most significant contribution was his role in founding the National Association for the Advancement of Colored People (NAACP). Established in 1909, the NAACP became a central force in the fight for civil rights, addressing issues like lynching, segregation, and voter disenfranchisement.

Du Bois was not only a founding member of the NAACP but also the editor of its monthly magazine, The Crisis. Under his leadership, The Crisis became a platform for showcasing African American literary talent and a powerful vehicle for promoting civil rights and social reform. It amplified the voices of African Americans and called attention to the racial injustices they faced.

The Niagara Movement

Before the NAACP, Du Bois was one of the leading figures in the Niagara Movement. This civil rights organization was a direct response to Washington's accommodationist policies and was committed to securing full civil liberties for African Americans and dismantling racial segregation. While the movement eventually dissolved and was overshadowed by the NAACP, its existence symbolized a clear call for a more assertive approach to racial equality.

Influence on African Americans and American Society

Du Bois' advocacy for civil rights, his belief in the power of higher education, and his critique of Washington's philosophy inspired many African Americans to challenge the status quo. His ideas influenced a generation of black leaders and intellectuals and laid the foundation for the civil rights movement of the 1950s and 1960s.

His work also resonated beyond the borders of the United States. His Pan-Africanist ideas inspired many leaders of the decolonization movement in Africa, and his writings continue to inform discussions about race and equality worldwide.

Despite the significant strides made in implementing Du Bois' ideas, they were not without their critics. In the next section, we will examine some of the critiques and limitations of his philosophy, providing a balanced perspective of his impact.

Section 4: Critiques and Limitations of Du Bois' Philosophy

Like any influential thinker, Du Bois faced criticism and scrutiny. This section examines these critiques and illuminates the potential limitations and challenges inherent in his philosophy.

Critiques from Contemporaries

Some of Du Bois' contemporaries criticized his approach as too idealistic and unattainable, particularly his concept of the 'Talented Tenth.' Critics argued that this strategy seemed to favor the intellectual elite at the expense of the majority of African Americans, who were poor and lacked access to higher education.

Additionally, his philosophy of full civil rights and political representation faced resistance from those who feared it could provoke backlash from white society, further deepening racial tensions. This fear was the driving force behind the more conservative, accommodationist stance of Washington and his supporters.

Modern Critiques

In recent years, some scholars have argued that Du Bois' focus on civil rights and political representation did not sufficiently address the economic disparities faced by African Americans. They suggest that without economic equality, political equality may be hollow.

Moreover, while Du Bois was an early advocate for women's rights, some have critiqued the gender dynamics of his 'Talented Tenth' concept, pointing out that it was primarily focused on developing male leadership. This critique underscores the need for intersectional approaches that consider both race and gender in the fight for equality.

Limitations and Challenges

Implementing Du Bois' philosophy also presents practical challenges. The systemic barriers to higher education for African Americans, for instance, make his vision of the 'Talented Tenth' difficult to achieve. Similarly, while his push for civil rights was undoubtedly necessary, it also faced staunch resistance and violent backlash, as evidenced by the long and arduous struggle of the Civil Rights Movement.

Despite these critiques and limitations, it's undeniable that Du Bois' ideas significantly influenced the fight for racial equality in the U.S. and beyond. His philosophy continues to resonate today, serving as a guiding light for those committed to challenging racial injustice. However, as we move forward, it's essential to consider these criticisms and limitations, refining and expanding upon his philosophy to meet contemporary needs.

By comparing and contrasting the philosophies of Washington and Du Bois, we can gain a more comprehensive understanding of the diverse strategies proposed to address racial inequality in America. This knowledge sets the stage for the discussion in the following chapter, where we consider a new approach that seeks to combine the strengths of these historical perspectives.

Chapter 3: Assessing the Impact:

Strengths and Weaknesses of Both Approaches." Comparative analysis of Washington's and Du Bois' philosophies.

Section 1: Comparative Overview of Washington and Du Bois

Two of the most influential figures in the history of African American civil rights, Booker T. Washington and W.E.B. Du Bois, emerged as leaders during times of intense racial segregation in America. Despite being champions of the same cause, they adopted significantly different strategies and ideologies in their struggle for equality and justice.

Born into slavery, Washington's experiences shaped his practical and somewhat conservative perspective. He advocated for economic self-reliance, vocational training, and gradual integration into society, which he believed would eventually lead to equal rights. On the other hand, Du Bois, a freeborn in the North and the first African American to earn a Ph.D. from Harvard, argued for immediate civil and political rights. He emphasized higher education and political activism as the path to racial equality.

Washington's philosophy, often characterized as accommodationist, urged African Americans to 'lift themselves by their bootstraps,' winning respect through hard work and economic prosperity. His vision of progress involved building racial solidarity and fostering a spirit of self-help within the African American community. He believed this would slowly, but surely, lead to integration and acceptance by white society.

Du Bois, meanwhile, posited that acceptance should not be begged for, but demanded. He envisioned an intellectual vanguard of African Americans—the 'Talented Tenth'—who, through higher education and political action, would lead the race to full civil rights. For Du Bois, accommodating to an unjust system was not a viable path to equality.

These different philosophies not only shaped the strategies of these two men but also significantly impacted the broader struggle for African American civil rights. The coming sections will delve deeper into the strengths and weaknesses of both these approaches, their enduring impacts, and how a synthesis of these philosophies might offer a novel perspective for our present era.

Section 2: The Strengths of Washington's and Du Bois' Approaches

Washington's philosophy, grounded in pragmatism, delivered immediate and tangible benefits. His emphasis on vocational skills and economic self-help was practical and achievable, providing African Americans with tools to lift themselves out of poverty and towards self-sufficiency. The Tuskegee Institute, which he founded, became a shining example of this, training generations of African Americans in trades and crafts. Washington's approach offered a means of survival and progress in a racially segregated and economically unequal society.

Moreover, Washington's philosophy advocated for racial solidarity, encouraging African Americans to build strong communities and institutions. His accommodationist stance, although critiqued, allowed African Americans to make significant socioeconomic strides without directly challenging the white-dominated status quo.

On the other hand, Du Bois' philosophy offered a more ambitious vision of progress. His advocacy for full civil rights and equal treatment under the law was a clarion call for justice that resonated deeply within the African American community and beyond. Du Bois argued that acceptance and equality should not be contingent on proving worth but should be fundamental human rights.

The emphasis on higher education that Du Bois championed provided the foundation for producing generations of African American leaders, intellectuals, and professionals. His belief in the "Talented Tenth," an educated elite that would lead and uplift the race, was instrumental in shaping the civil rights movements of the 20th century.

In his fight for equality, Du Bois also laid the groundwork for international solidarity among people of African descent. His Pan-Africanist ideals connected the struggle for civil rights in America with global movements against colonialism and racism, widening the scope of the battle for racial equality.

Both Washington's pragmatism and Du Bois' idealism offered valuable pathways to progress, each with its strengths suited to the challenges of their respective eras. However, neither approach was without its limitations, as we will explore in the next section.

Section 3: The Weaknesses of Washington's and Du Bois' Approaches

Despite the strengths of Washington's pragmatic philosophy, it fell short of addressing the systemic racism entrenched in American society. His accommodationist stance, while avoiding direct confrontation with the white-dominated status quo, did not challenge the fundamental inequalities African Americans faced. This strategy of self-help and economic upliftment without political agitation for civil rights was seen by many, including Du Bois, as a tacit acceptance of second-class citizenship. Additionally, Washington's focus on industrial education risked pigeonholing African Americans into a limited range of occupations, potentially reinforcing racial stereotypes rather than dismantling them.

Similarly, Du Bois' approach, while powerful in its call for full civil rights, also faced significant criticisms. His emphasis on a 'Talented Tenth,' an educated elite that would lead the African American community, risked neglecting the needs of the majority of African Americans who lacked access to higher education. This strategy, though designed to uplift the entire community, could inadvertently exacerbate class divisions within the African American community itself. Furthermore, Du Bois' insistence on immediate civil rights, while morally unassailable, was often met with violent resistance, highlighting the perils of confronting a deeply unjust system head-on.

These weaknesses are not mentioned to diminish the immense contributions of these two luminaries but to further our understanding of their philosophies. By recognizing the limitations of these past strategies, we can better navigate the complexities of the current socio-economic landscape and chart a more inclusive and comprehensive path towards progress, which we will explore in the next chapter.

Section 4: A Modern Perspective: Relevance in Today's World

Even over a century later, the philosophies of both Washington and Du Bois continue to resonate, speaking volumes about their relevance in our modern world. Their perspectives on racial progress, education, and economic empowerment provide a powerful lens to view and address present-day issues of racial inequality, educational disparity, and economic injustice.

Washington's emphasis on economic self-help and vocational education remains relevant, particularly in a world where the socio-economic gap continues to widen. His ideas about acquiring practical skills for economic upliftment echo in contemporary discussions on the value of vocational education and the need to equip individuals with skills that align with market demands. In a society where wealth inequality is a stark reality, Washington's philosophy underlines the importance of financial literacy and entrepreneurship as tools for economic empowerment.

Meanwhile, Du Bois' fight for civil rights and his emphasis on higher education resonate strongly in the current climate where racial injustice and educational disparities are at the forefront of societal discourse. His insistence on political agitation for equal rights echoes in contemporary movements like Black Lives Matter, advocating for systemic change and justice. The idea of the 'Talented Tenth,' though critiqued, carries forward in the push for broader access to higher education, especially for marginalized communities.

However, the lessons from the limitations of their philosophies are equally important. They remind us of the need for a comprehensive strategy that combines the pursuit of economic self-reliance, high-quality education for all, and the relentless fight against systemic injustice.

In the next part of this book, we will pivot from analyzing the past and delve into the present and future. We'll explore how we can synthesize the lessons from these historical philosophies and inform a new approach centered around innovation, entrepreneurship, and equal opportunity. We'll explore the potential of this 'Third Path' to uplift not just the African American community but all communities striving for progress and equity.

Section 5: Setting the Stage for a Third Path

Our exploration of the legacies of Booker T. Washington and W.E.B. Du Bois illuminates the complex dynamics of racial progress and economic empowerment. Washington's focus on economic self-help and practical education offered tangible avenues for African Americans to progress, yet it did not directly challenge the systemic racial inequalities entrenched in American society. On the other hand, Du Bois advocated for civil rights and higher education, but his focus on the 'Talented Tenth' may have inadvertently overlooked the majority of African Americans who couldn't access these opportunities.

This raises a pivotal question: Can we find a 'third path,' an approach that addresses the unique challenges of the present era while acknowledging the historical wisdom of both leaders? Is there a route that bridges the strengths of self-reliance with systemic change, vocational skills with higher education, and economic empowerment with political representation?

As industrialist John D. Rockefeller reportedly stated, "I want a nation of workers, not thinkers." But what if we challenge this notion? What if, instead, we aspire to nurture a nation of thinkers and creators, not merely workers? In a world continually reshaped by technology, many traditional jobs are disappearing. Instead, creative, innovative roles are stepping into the limelight.

As an educator, a pastor, a business owner, and an African American with several higher degrees, I understand the crucial interplay between higher education, practical skills, and entrepreneurship. It is with this perspective that I propose the 'third path'—a blend of innovative thinking, higher education, and entrepreneurship that aims to empower individuals to not only navigate but also shape the future.

The 'third path' encourages us to envision a more comprehensive approach towards racial and economic equality. How can we create a culture where everyone, regardless of their race or background, can become innovators and creators? What practical steps can we take to foster entrepreneurship within our communities?

In the subsequent parts of this book, we will delve into these questions. We will explore how we can leverage the power of higher education, creativity, and innovation to foster a nation of thinkers and creators. We will also outline the vision for an African American STEAM & Entrepreneurship Academy, a place where these principles can be put into action.

By doing this, we strive for a world where every individual has the tools to shape their own destiny and contribute meaningfully to society. This is not merely an academic discourse but a call to action—an invitation to join the journey of the 'third path.' As we chart this course, we aren't just transcending the dichotomy of Washington vs. Du Bois; we are shaping a new narrative that harnesses the best of both philosophies for the good of humanity. And as we take this journey, let's remember to guide our efforts with love—for it is love that truly transforms.

So, are you ready to embark on this 'third path'? Ready to join the movement towards a dynamic, inclusive future that benefits all of humanity? If so, turn the page and let's begin this extraordinary journey together.

Part II: The Modern Context

Chapter 4: 21st Century Challenges:

Why We Need a New Approach." Examination of modern societal and economic challenges.

Section 1: The Lingering Legacy of Racial Inequality

The journey through the annals of history paints a vivid picture of the legacy of racial inequality, a legacy that reaches from the times of Washington and Du Bois and extends its tentacles into our present day. In light of this history, we must ask ourselves: how has this legacy been perpetuated in our own time, and what does current research tell us about the state of racial inequality today?

In the era of Washington and Du Bois, racial inequality was explicit and codified into the laws governing the land. While the laws may have changed, a 2017 study from the Economic Policy Institute reveals that the wage gap between black and white workers in the US is wider today than it was in 1979. What could be driving this persistent disparity?

One potential answer lies in redlining, a practice with roots in the 1930s. Redlining involved government policies that discriminated against neighborhoods with high minority populations, deeming them risky and undesirable for home loans. The National Community Reinvestment Coalition (NCRC) reported in 2018 that three out of four neighborhoods marked "hazardous" in redlining maps eight decades ago continue to struggle economically. How has this historical practice influenced racial disparities in homeownership and wealth in modern times?

School segregation, too, plays a significant role in this ongoing narrative. Despite the landmark Brown v. Board of Education decision in 1954, a 2019 UCLA Civil Rights Project report showed that many schools today remain segregated in practice. What impact does this de facto segregation have on educational opportunities for students of color?

Mass incarceration is another glaring example of modern racial disparity. According to the NAACP, African Americans are incarcerated at more than five times the rate of whites. What are the systemic issues contributing to this problem, and how can they be addressed?

Together, these elements—redlining, school segregation, and mass incarceration—form the sinews of the enduring legacy of racial inequality. They underscore the urgency of our quest for racial justice. To address these deeply entrenched inequalities, we must consider innovative, informed, and compassionate approaches that move us closer to a society where everyone, regardless of race, has the opportunity to flourish. What might these new strategies look like, and how can they build on the work of past leaders like

Washington and Du Bois? The exploration of these questions forms the crux of our discussion moving forward.

Section 2: The Reality of Economic Inequality

While the battle against racial disparity rages on, another equally significant struggle persists concurrently: the battle against economic inequality. Economic disparities can be difficult to fully comprehend without clear numbers to illuminate the truth. Thus, it begs the question: what is the current state of economic inequality in our society?

The hard data is both illuminating and sobering. A study published by the Pew Research Center in 2020 reports that the wealth gap between America's richest and poorest families more than doubled from 1989 to 2016. But what does this gap look like? How does it translate to daily living and opportunities for the individuals and families caught in the widening divide?

To answer these questions, consider this: the wealthiest 5% of American families had 248 times as much wealth as the median family in 2016, up from 112 times in 1989. How do these staggering wealth disparities impact the quality of life and the opportunities available to those on the lower end of the economic spectrum?

These inequalities become even more pronounced when we consider racial and ethnic lines. A 2021 report from the Brookings Institution reveals that the net worth of a typical white family is nearly ten times greater than that of a Black family. With such a chasm in wealth distribution, how can we ensure equitable opportunities for all?

The story of economic inequality is also told through income gaps and unemployment rates. According to a report from the Bureau of Labor Statistics, as of May 2023, the unemployment rate for Black Americans is nearly double the national average. Moreover, the Economic Policy Institute's research in 2021 showed that Black workers are paid on average only 73.4% of what their white counterparts earn.

These stark realities of economic inequality underscore the urgency of crafting new approaches to combat these deeply entrenched disparities. Such approaches must not only ensure the availability of jobs but also promote fair pay, economic mobility, and wealth creation. As we continue this exploration, we ask: how can the philosophies of Washington and Du Bois guide us in addressing these pressing challenges, and where do their strategies need to evolve? By asking these questions, we hope to chart a course towards a future where economic equality is more than a distant dream, but a tangible reality.

Section 3: Inequalities in the Tech Era

As we navigate the digital age, an insidious development has occurred, amplifying pre-existing racial and economic inequalities. Today, we confront a new kind of disparity: the digital divide. This term refers to the gap between those who have ready access to computers and the internet, and those who do not. And why is this divide relevant in our exploration of modern inequalities?

According to a Pew Research Center study conducted in 2021, 7% of U.S. adults stated that they do not use the internet. For individuals in rural areas, those with lower incomes, and older adults, the number rises. Without internet access, these individuals lack the necessary tools to participate fully in a digital society, potentially missing out on opportunities for learning, employment, and social connection.

The tech era has not only brought the digital divide but also a striking lack of diversity within the tech industry itself. According to a 2020 report by the National Urban League titled "State of Black America," Black people make up only 7.9% of the tech industry, compared to the 13.4% they represent in the total U.S. population. This disparity prompts the question: what barriers prevent a more diverse representation within this crucial industry, and how can they be overcome?

Lastly, technological advancements, though promising, have often inadvertently widened socio-economic gaps. For instance, automation threatens jobs traditionally held by low-income workers, while higher-income professions are less likely to be impacted. A 2020 report from the Brookings Institution reveals that roughly a quarter of U.S. employment (36 million jobs) is highly exposed to automation. How can we ensure that the technological revolution uplifts all communities, rather than exacerbating current inequalities?

The issues outlined in this section paint a daunting picture of the challenges that the tech era presents to marginalized communities. However, by recognizing these challenges, we can begin to devise strategies that utilize technology as a tool for leveling the playing field, rather than furthering disparities. As we seek to reconcile the philosophies of Washington and Du Bois with our current context, we ask: how can we foster an environment where technology empowers rather than excludes?

Section 4: The Impact of COVID-19

The global outbreak of COVID-19 has deepened many of the divides that we've already examined, laying bare the vulnerabilities of disadvantaged communities. This section explores the multifaceted impacts of the pandemic, with a focus on disparities in health outcomes, the economic fallout, and the challenges of remote learning.

According to a report by the Centers for Disease Control and Prevention (CDC), racial and ethnic minority groups were significantly more likely to be hospitalized or die from COVID-19. The CDC attributes these disparities to long-standing systemic health and social inequities. Could these disproportionate health outcomes have been avoided with earlier interventions?

The pandemic has not only had a significant impact on physical health, but also on economic wellbeing. A study from the University of California Santa Cruz showed that nearly half of Black-owned small businesses had been wiped out by the end of April 2020. The question here is, how can we better support these businesses in times of crisis and help rebuild these economic lifelines?

Additionally, the pandemic triggered a dramatic shift to remote learning. The National Education Association points out that the transition has been particularly challenging for under-resourced schools, with students struggling to access necessary technology and facing difficulties learning at home. In light of this, what steps can be taken to ensure equal access to quality education, regardless of socio-economic background or location?

The COVID-19 pandemic has cast a glaring spotlight on societal disparities. The challenge now is to apply these lessons in a way that rectifies these injustices. As we move forward, we must question how to prevent such drastic disparities in future crises.

Section 5: The Perseverance of Communities

Despite the immense challenges faced by marginalized communities, it is essential to highlight their resilience and capacity for innovation in the face of adversity. This section celebrates examples of community-led initiatives and triumphs that demonstrate how perseverance can drive change.

Take, for instance, the incredible resurgence of Black-owned businesses despite the devastating impacts of COVID-19. A study by Guidant Financial reported a significant increase in Black entrepreneurship, with 30% of all small businesses being Black-owned in 2020, up from 15% in 2019. What can we learn from this surge in entrepreneurship? How can we better support these businesses to ensure their sustainability?

In the realm of education, communities have rallied to mitigate the impact of remote learning. One remarkable example is the 'Digital Navigators' program in Washington D.C., a community-led initiative that provides technical support and devices for students struggling with online schooling. What other community-led initiatives could be implemented to assist under-resourced schools during these challenging times?

Across the globe, communities have rallied, supporting each other in ways that have been both innovative and inspiring. Despite systemic inequalities, these stories of resilience offer hope and can guide us in crafting solutions that address the unique needs of diverse communities.

In every adversity lies an opportunity for growth and change. This section prompts us to ask, how can we harness this resilience and community spirit to create a more inclusive and equitable society?

Section 6: Setting the Stage for the Third Path - Extended Version

As we bring this section to a close, we highlight the pressing need for an innovative and dynamic approach, one that synthesizes the past and embraces the future. This necessity stems from the lingering racial disparities, the realities of economic imbalances, and the novel challenges that technological advancements and the COVID-19 pandemic present. In the face of such issues, a new path, a Third Path, becomes a crucial consideration.

Unlike Booker T. Washington's philosophy, which hinged heavily on self-help and practical skills, or W.E.B. Du Bois' focus on civil rights and higher education, this Third Path seeks to navigate a middle course, harmonizing elements from both their philosophies. It also seeks to push the envelope further, incorporating an understanding of the unique challenges and opportunities of our present era. This path must negotiate systemic barriers while preparing individuals with the necessary tools, skills, and mindsets to flourish in an evolving world. The question remains: what might this Third

Path look like, and how can it be flexible, comprehensive, and responsive to change?

Imagine a path where we foster a culture of creativity, critical thinking, and innovation. These characteristics are crucial for the new generation of leaders and problem solvers. With the rise of artificial intelligence and other technological advancements, jobs that exist today may become obsolete tomorrow. We need thinkers, creators, and innovators who can adapt to these changes and find solutions to new problems.

Furthermore, think about the transformative power of social entrepreneurship. Research shows that such ventures can significantly contribute to closing wealth gaps while simultaneously fostering innovation and addressing social needs. The Third Path could draw from these insights and foster an entrepreneurial spirit that disrupts systemic inequality.

But it's not just about creating businesses. It's about cultivating a mindset that sees possibilities where others see problems, opportunities where others see obstacles. It's about empowering individuals to become architects of their future and catalysts for community transformation. It's about creating a nation of thinkers and creators, not mere workers in jobs that may no longer exist in the future.

Such a path is not an easy one. It requires us to rethink our educational systems, our policies, and our societal structures. It requires us to confront difficult truths and to challenge the status quo. But if we can do this, we can pave the way towards a more equitable and prosperous future.

The Third Path beckons us towards a fresh exploration, one that harnesses the strength and resilience of marginalized communities, the transformative potential of innovation, and the necessity for systemic change. As we continue our journey through this book, we invite you to imagine, question, and engage with us as we outline and traverse this Third Path.

Chapter 5: The Rise of Entrepreneurship:

A Global Phenomenon." Overview of the growth and impact of entrepreneurship.

Section 1: Understanding Entrepreneurship

Understanding entrepreneurship entails much more than simply associating it with the act of starting a business. The real essence of entrepreneurship lies in the mindset, actions, and motives of individuals who see a problem as an opportunity to create value.

The term 'entrepreneur' has roots in the 18th-century French verb 'entreprendre', which means 'to undertake.' While it was Richard Cantillon who first introduced the term 'entrepreneur' in the world of economics in 1730, it was Jean-Baptiste Say who popularized it. Say defined an entrepreneur as an 'adventurer' who takes risks to create innovative products or services and bring them to the market (1).

In today's world, entrepreneurship is synonymous with elements such as innovation, risk-taking, and opportunity recognition.

According to Schumpeter (1942), entrepreneurship is all about creative destruction - replacing old and inefficient structures with new, more productive ones (2).

Entrepreneurship plays a critical role in the economy. It's been found that new and young companies are the primary source of job creation in the American economy (3). Beyond job creation, entrepreneurs innovate, bring new products and ideas to the market, disrupt traditional business models, and contribute to the dynamism of the economy.

Successful entrepreneurs exhibit certain key characteristics. They are typically self-reliant, passionate, resilient, and extremely motivated. They are not afraid of failure, have strong networking abilities, are flexible, and possess strong decision-making capabilities (4).

Now, think about this: What are some examples of problems in your community that could be opportunities for entrepreneurship? How would you use entrepreneurial thinking to approach these issues?

Section 2: Entrepreneurship: The Global Surge

The recent decades have witnessed an unprecedented surge in entrepreneurship around the globe. According to the Global Entrepreneurship Monitor, in 2019, an estimated 582 million entrepreneurs were operating businesses worldwide (1). But what's driving this massive entrepreneurial wave?

Technology undoubtedly plays a key role. The digital revolution has reduced entry barriers across industries, making it easier than ever for individuals to start businesses. From e-commerce platforms to digital marketing tools, technology has opened up new avenues for entrepreneurs to reach customers and scale their operations (2).

Another driver of this entrepreneurship boom is the shift in economic dynamics. In the face of economic downturns and job instability, more individuals are turning to entrepreneurship as a means of creating their own economic security. Moreover, there's been a growing recognition of the role small businesses play in driving economic growth and innovation, leading to increased support and incentives for entrepreneurship (3).

Policy and cultural shifts have also been instrumental. Governments worldwide have been introducing policies and programs to foster entrepreneurial ecosystems, from providing financial incentives and easing regulations to offering training programs. Simultaneously, there's been a cultural shift, with entrepreneurship being increasingly celebrated and perceived as a desirable career path (4).

On a broader level, the rise of entrepreneurship reflects a desire for autonomy, personal fulfillment, and the opportunity to make an impact. As society becomes more receptive to new ideas and innovation, entrepreneurship provides a vehicle for individuals to express their creativity, solve problems, and contribute to their communities.

Now, consider this: What impact do you think this global surge in entrepreneurship could have on your community? On your life? What opportunities could it create, and what challenges could it present?

Section 3: The Impact of Entrepreneurship on Economies

Entrepreneurship, a powerful engine of economic growth, has far-reaching impacts on economies worldwide. The role of entrepreneurs extends beyond merely establishing new businesses. They create jobs, drive innovation, foster competition, and contribute to wealth distribution.

Firstly, entrepreneurs are job creators. According to the U.S. Small Business Administration, small businesses have generated 64% of net new jobs over the past two decades (1). Beyond the direct employment they provide, startups also indirectly create jobs through increased demand for related businesses and services. For example, a new restaurant opening can lead to increased demand for local farmers, decorators, and delivery services.

Secondly, entrepreneurship drives innovation. Entrepreneurs introduce new products, services, and technologies, pushing existing companies to innovate or lose market share. In Silicon Valley, for instance, the dynamic startup culture has produced a myriad of technological advancements that have reshaped industries worldwide (2).

Thirdly, entrepreneurs foster competition. The entrance of new businesses challenges incumbents, prevents monopolies, and often results in better quality products and services. Case in point, the emergence of digital banking startups has disrupted traditional banking, leading to improved customer experiences and financial inclusivity (3).

Lastly, entrepreneurship can contribute to wealth distribution. While entrepreneurship often results in wealth accumulation for successful business owners, it also provides opportunities for others to create wealth. Many tech companies, for instance, have produced not only billionaire founders but also thousands of millionaire employees through stock options.

Consider the case of M-Pesa in Kenya. This mobile money transfer service, started by Vodafone, has transformed the economic landscape by providing financial services to millions previously unbanked. It has also stimulated entrepreneurial activity and job creation in the country (4).

However, the impacts of entrepreneurship aren't always universally positive. Questions arise: Can entrepreneurship deepen wealth inequality when only a few entrepreneurs amass great fortunes? Do all innovations result in net positive impacts for society?

In essence, the influence of entrepreneurship on economies is profound, complex, and multifaceted. Understanding these impacts helps shape policies and practices to harness entrepreneurship's potential benefits and mitigate its potential drawbacks.

Create Section 4: Entrepreneurship and Social Change

Entrepreneurship's role extends beyond economic realms, becoming a powerful agent for social change. Entrepreneurs can drive social progress, create innovative solutions to social issues, and promote community development and environmental sustainability. This shift towards purposeful business is encapsulated in the growing field of social entrepreneurship.

Social entrepreneurship is a blend of business acumen and social purpose. It involves creating sustainable business models that address unmet social needs, seeking both financial returns and social impact. Muhammad Yunus's Grameen Bank is a classic example of social entrepreneurship. This microfinance organization provides small loans to poor individuals, primarily women, who would otherwise lack access to financial services, thus combating poverty and empowering women (1).

Entrepreneurs also contribute significantly to community development. By starting businesses, they stimulate local economies, create jobs, and often invest in community projects. For instance, Hamdi Ulukaya, the founder of Chobani, has revitalized local communities in the US by creating jobs and implementing profit-sharing programs with his employees (2).

Further, in the face of environmental degradation and climate change, many entrepreneurs are stepping up to the plate. They are developing innovative solutions for renewable energy, waste reduction, and sustainable agriculture, marking the rise of eco-entrepreneurship. Elon Musk's Tesla and SolarCity are prominent examples of businesses driving environmental sustainability through innovative products and services (3).

However, the relationship between entrepreneurship and social change is complex. Not all entrepreneurial activities lead to positive social outcomes, and businesses can sometimes exacerbate social problems. Furthermore, social entrepreneurs often face unique challenges, such as balancing the dual goals of profit and impact and securing funding.

In essence, while entrepreneurs can undoubtedly contribute to social change, it is crucial to understand the nuanced dynamics of this relationship. By doing so, we can better encourage and support those entrepreneurs who strive to create not only successful businesses but also a better world.

Discussion Questions:

1. Can businesses balance the pursuit of profits and social impact?
2. What are the potential challenges and pitfalls of social entrepreneurship?
3. How can we support entrepreneurs in driving social change?

Section 5: Challenges and Opportunities in Entrepreneurship

Entrepreneurship, despite its many benefits, has its challenges. It requires a delicate balance of risk and reward, innovation and market understanding, resilience, and adaptability. For many entrepreneurs, especially those from marginalized communities, these challenges can often seem insurmountable.

One of the most significant challenges entrepreneurs face is accessing capital. Traditional sources of funding, such as bank loans, venture capital, and angel investments, often remain elusive, particularly for minority and women entrepreneurs. Research indicates that women-led startups receive only 2.2% of all venture capital funding, while Black entrepreneurs receive a mere 1% (1). This lack of capital restricts their ability to start and grow businesses, thereby limiting the potential economic and social impact of their entrepreneurial activities.

Market competition is another major challenge. In today's hyper-connected world, businesses must compete with local rivals and companies across the globe. This intense competition requires entrepreneurs to constantly innovate, adapt, and stay ahead of market trends, which can be particularly challenging for new and small businesses with limited resources.

Regulatory hurdles also pose significant challenges. Navigating the complexities of business laws, tax codes, and regulatory compliance can be time-consuming and daunting for entrepreneurs. In some cases, regulatory barriers may even stifle innovation and discourage entrepreneurship.

Despite these challenges, entrepreneurship also presents numerous opportunities. The rise of digital technologies has significantly lowered the barriers to entrepreneurship. It has never been easier to start a business, reach global markets, and innovate at scale. Technology has also enabled new forms of entrepreneurship, such as social entrepreneurship and digital entrepreneurship, opening up new avenues for impact.

The growing support for entrepreneurship from governments, corporations, and communities presents another opportunity. Across the world, policies are being implemented to foster entrepreneurial ecosystems, support startups, and stimulate innovation. This supportive environment, coupled with increasing societal recognition of the value of entrepreneurship, creates a favorable landscape for aspiring entrepreneurs.

As we move towards discussing the Third Path in the next chapter, it is crucial to consider both these challenges and opportunities. The Third Path, as we envision it, is not simply about promoting entrepreneurship. It's about reimagining entrepreneurship in a way that addresses the systemic barriers, leverages the opportunities of the modern world, and ultimately, contributes to a more equitable and resilient society.

Questions for Reflection:

1. How can we ensure that entrepreneurship is inclusive and accessible to all, irrespective of their gender, race, or socio-economic background?
2. How can entrepreneurs leverage technology to overcome market competition and create differentiated value?
3. What role can policy play in mitigating the challenges faced by entrepreneurs and fostering a vibrant entrepreneurial ecosystem?

Create Part III: The Third Path

Chapter 6: Redefining the Vision:

Merging the Old with the New."

"Section 1: Connecting the Past and the Present

In connecting the past and the present, we revisit the enduring philosophies of Booker T. Washington and W.E.B. Du Bois, two figures whose ideas have shaped the discourse on racial and economic equality (Harlan, 1983; Lewis, 2009). Washington advocated for self-help, practical skills, and economic upliftment for African Americans, fostering immediate and tangible benefits (Washington, 1901). Du Bois, meanwhile, championed the cause of civil rights, higher education, and political representation, laying the groundwork for long-term systemic change (Du Bois, 1903).

In the 21st century, the 4Cs—critical thinking, communication, collaboration, and creativity—have gained recognition as key skills needed for success in information and technology-rich societies (Partnership for 21st Century Learning, 2019). Reflecting on Washington's and Du Bois' ideas, it's evident that these early advocates for African American progress were, in many ways, underscoring the importance of these skills.

Washington's focus on practical skills development resonates with today's emphasis on 'learning to learn'—a concept central to critical thinking and problem-solving (Wagner, 2008). For instance, when one learns a new software, it's not merely about understanding its current functions but learning how to adapt as the software updates or changes.

Similarly, Du Bois' insistence on higher education aligns with the modern focus on creativity and innovation in knowledge creation (Rampersad, 2019). Higher education often provides the space and tools to question existing knowledge and generate new ideas.

Both leaders' visions also align with the current emphasis on information, media, and technology literacy. They stressed the importance of staying informed and using available resources to further individual and community growth. Today, this translates into the need to navigate and utilize digital tools and platforms effectively (Buckingham, 2007). For example, understanding how to discern credible sources online helps individuals make informed decisions about their lives and communities.

By drawing on these historical philosophies and integrating them with modern entrepreneurial thinking, we can create a new educational and societal paradigm. This paradigm would equip individuals not only with the skills to excel in their careers but also with the ability to contribute positively to their communities and the broader society. For example, an entrepreneur with a solid grasp of the 4Cs would not only be able to grow their business but also identify and address the needs of their community.

"Section 2: The Merger: Education, Entrepreneurship, and Empowerment

The merger of higher education, entrepreneurial thinking, and the advocacy for rights and representation forms a powerful synergy capable of inspiring individual empowerment and societal transformation (Kuratko, 2019). This integrated approach has the potential to nurture individuals who are not only economically self-sufficient but also actively engaged in their communities and society at large.

Higher education serves as a bedrock in this fusion by providing a space where critical thinking, creativity, and collaborative skills—essential elements of the 4Cs—are honed (Morrison, 2019). These skills serve as the foundation upon which entrepreneurial thinking and advocacy for rights and representation are built.

Question for Reflection: How have your educational experiences equipped you with the 4Cs, and how have these skills influenced your career or entrepreneurial journey?

Entrepreneurial thinking adds an innovative and pragmatic layer to this approach. It encourages individuals to identify opportunities, take calculated risks, and create value—be it economic, social, or cultural (Coulter, 2013). This mindset is not confined to business ventures; it also applies to social initiatives and policy advocacy, which can bring about systemic change.

Discussion Point: Can you think of a social issue in your community that could benefit from an entrepreneurial approach? How might you apply entrepreneurial thinking to address this issue?

Advocacy for rights and representation, a cause championed by Du Bois, remains just as crucial in the 21st century. It ensures that all voices, especially those from marginalized communities, are heard and that these diverse perspectives contribute to policy-making, social change, and community development (Takaki, 2008).

Think about this: What steps can individuals and communities take to ensure their voices are heard in decision-making processes, and how can this contribute to societal change?

Lastly, the emphasis on life and career skills such as flexibility, initiative, social and cross-cultural skills, productivity, and leadership comes to the fore (Trilling & Fadel, 2009). These skills are instrumental in navigating today's rapidly changing, interconnected world and driving personal, community, and societal advancement.

Reflection Question: How do life and career skills like flexibility, initiative, and leadership factor into your personal and professional life?

"Section 3: Case Studies: The Third Path in Action

To truly grasp the potential of the Third Path approach—merging education, entrepreneurship, and empowerment—it's crucial to examine real-world implementations. Therefore, we delve deeper into two cases from Bangladesh and Brazil that have been successful in stimulating change by embracing this integrated approach.

Our first case takes us to rural Bangladesh, where poverty and a lack of access to traditional banking services pose significant barriers to economic development. Enter Grameen Bank, a revolutionary institution founded by economist Muhammad Yunus (Yunus, 2003). Understanding that these underserved populations were not "unbankable", Yunus developed a microcredit model that provides small loans to those who don't qualify for traditional banking services, primarily women. By doing so, Grameen Bank fosters entrepreneurship among individuals who previously had no access to start-up capital.

But Grameen Bank goes beyond mere lending. They also offer educational programs, instilling crucial business skills such as basic accounting, inventory management, and market research among their borrowers. This education component enables the recipients to effectively use the microloans to develop sustainable businesses. In essence, Grameen Bank not only offers financial resources but also promotes economic empowerment through education and entrepreneurship, illustrating a successful application of the Third Path.

Discussion Point: How has the Grameen Bank model managed to intertwine education, entrepreneurship, and empowerment? How could similar principles be applied in your community?

The next example transports us to the favelas of Brazil. Here, the problem is twofold: systemic social exclusion leading to a lack of opportunities, and a negative cycle of violence and crime. Responding to this dire need, AfroReggae Cultural Group emerged as a beacon of hope (Vieira & Granado, 2011). This organization harnesses the power of culture and arts to engage the youth of the favelas, diverting them away from crime and towards constructive outlets.

AfroReggae offers education and training in areas such as music, dance, and media production, cultivating creative skills and creating potential career paths in the process. It also operates as an entrepreneurial venture, generating income from performances, workshops, and merchandise sales that fund their initiatives. Beyond this, AfroReggae advocates for the rights of favela residents, lobbying for better public services, and working to change societal perceptions of these marginalized communities.

Reflect on this: How does the AfroReggae model embody the Third Path, and what impacts has it had on the community? Can you think of a similar situation where art and entrepreneurship could intersect to drive positive social change?

Both Grameen Bank and AfroReggae underline the transformative potential of the Third Path. These organizations showcase how providing education, fostering entrepreneurial thinking, and championing empowerment can help individuals and communities overcome significant challenges, innovate, and stimulate social progress.

Reflection Question: Looking at these two case studies, how can you envision the principles of the Third Path being applied to address specific challenges in your community?

"Section 4: Looking Ahead: Embracing the Third Path

Embracing the Third Path is more than just acknowledging the intertwined nature of education, entrepreneurship, and empowerment; it requires active participation, tenacity, and creativity from each of us. As we have seen in the preceding case studies, the effects of this approach can be transformative, leading to social change, community resilience, and economic progress (Yunus, 2003; Vieira & Granado, 2011).

However, the journey toward this integrated approach isn't without its challenges. Overcoming the systemic barriers that stand in the way will require collective action and relentless advocacy. So, how can we, as individuals and communities, contribute to this journey?

For individuals, the journey begins with self-development. This includes fostering the 4Cs—critical thinking, communication, collaboration, and creativity (Partnership for 21st Century Learning, 2019)—and leveraging these skills in our personal and professional lives. We should also embrace lifelong learning, constantly seeking opportunities to expand our knowledge and skills.

Reflection Question: How can you cultivate and utilize the 4Cs in your life?

Moreover, becoming more informed about the societal issues that affect us and the world around us is essential. This will equip us with the knowledge needed to engage in informed advocacy, an essential component of the Third Path.

Discussion Point: What are some societal issues you care deeply about, and how can you become a more informed advocate for them?

For communities, it's important to foster an environment that values education, nurtures entrepreneurial thinking, and supports empowerment. This might involve investing in educational resources, facilitating workshops and forums to share knowledge and ideas, and advocating for policies that support entrepreneurs and marginalized groups.

Think About This: What resources or initiatives could your community implement to foster a Third Path environment?

Looking ahead, our vision is a society where everyone has access to quality education, where entrepreneurial thinking is nurtured, and where empowerment is a reality for all, irrespective of their race, gender, or socio-economic status. This vision aligns with global efforts towards achieving the Sustainable Development Goals, particularly in the areas of quality education, decent work and economic growth, and reduced inequalities (United Nations, 2015).

As we close this chapter, we urge each reader to reflect on the roles they can play in realizing this vision. Let the Third Path not just be a concept but a shared mission, propelling us towards a future of equality, prosperity, and resilience.

Final Reflection: How can you contribute to making the Third Path a reality in your community?

Chapter 7: Entrepreneurship as Empowerment:

Stories of Success

Introduction:

In this chapter, we delve into the inspiring stories of successful Black entrepreneurs. Each narrative embodies the essence of the Third Path, shedding light on how their unwavering resilience, entrepreneurial spirit, and application of 21st-century skills created ripple effects that extended beyond personal success to community upliftment and societal change.

Madam C.J. Walker

Born Sarah Breedlove in 1867, Madam C.J. Walker grew up in a cabin on a cotton plantation as the child of former slaves. After suffering from a scalp ailment resulting in hair loss, she saw a need for better hair care products for Black women. With only $1.50 to her name, she started experimenting with homemade remedies. She faced countless trials, financial constraints, and a society skeptical of a Black woman entrepreneur. Yet, she persisted. Walker tirelessly marketed her products door-to-door, trained sales agents, and eventually established a factory and a beauty school. Her approach was revolutionary for the time, reflecting the 21st-century skills of creativity, critical thinking, and problem-solving. She became an advocate for Black women's economic independence, proving how resilience and entrepreneurial thinking can overcome adversity.

Robert F. Smith

Raised during the civil rights era, Robert F. Smith developed an early interest in technology. He encountered significant obstacles in his career, including racial discrimination. However, Smith perceived these challenges as opportunities to innovate. After a successful career in investment banking at Goldman Sachs, Smith founded Vista Equity Partners in 2000. Despite initial skepticism from investors, he maintained his focus on investing in software companies. His entrepreneurial journey, characterized by strategic thinking, adaptability, and a solid understanding of technology's role in modern business, eventually paid off. Today, Vista manages equity capital commitments of over $73 billion and oversees a portfolio of over 60 software companies, making it one of the world's most successful private equity firms.

Oprah Winfrey

Born into poverty in rural Mississippi, Oprah Winfrey rose to become a media mogul through determination and grit. Her career in media didn't start smoothly. At her first television job, she was deemed "unfit for TV." However, she did not let this setback define her. Instead, Winfrey used her empathetic communication style to her advantage when she moved to Chicago to host AM Chicago. The show, later renamed 'The Oprah Winfrey Show,' revolutionized the TV talk show format. She demonstrated exceptional interpersonal, cross-cultural skills, leadership, and emotional intelligence, paving the way for her unparalleled success in the media industry.

Janice Bryant Howroyd

Janice Bryant Howroyd's journey from her small hometown in North Carolina to CEO of a billion-dollar company, ActOne Group, is a testament to her tenacity. After moving to Los Angeles in 1976, she founded the ActOne Group with a $900 loan from her mother. Despite the harsh business landscape, she held firm to her vision. Howroyd's journey was fraught with challenges such as capital constraints, market competition, and racial discrimination. However, she used these adversities to fuel her ambition rather than hinder it. Today, her company is a global enterprise that provides employment, workforce management, and procurement solutions.

Tristan Walker

Tristan Walker, the founder of Walker & Company Brands, was raised in the projects of Queens, New York. Despite facing the challenges of poverty and violence in his neighborhood, he held onto his ambition. He put his critical thinking and problem-solving skills to work and managed to earn scholarships to prestigious schools. Later, as an entrepreneur, he noticed the lack of grooming products tailored for people of color. This led to the creation of Bevel, a shaving system designed specifically for Black men. The success of Bevel demonstrates the power of spotting unmet market needs and devising innovative solutions.

Section 6: Richelieu Dennis

Richelieu Dennis grew up in Liberia and experienced the harsh realities of war before migrating to the United States. Once in the U.S., Dennis and his roommate noticed a gap in the market for products catering to the specific needs of African women's skin and hair. Despite having limited resources, they started making and selling their natural products. Their venture, Sundial Brands, creators of Nubian Heritage and Shea Moisture, faced numerous rejections and funding difficulties. However, Dennis's perseverance, creativity, and commitment to his mission led the company to massive success.

Sheila Johnson

Sheila Johnson, co-founder of Black Entertainment Television (BET) and CEO of Salamander Hotels and Resorts, transitioned from a career in music to entrepreneurship. Despite encountering gender and racial barriers in her journey, Johnson used her inherent creativity and resilience to build BET alongside her then-husband. She later diversified into hospitality, where she leveraged her understanding of luxury consumers to build a successful hotel chain. Johnson exemplifies how transferable skills and a willingness to venture into uncharted territories can lead to entrepreneurial success.

Aliko Dangote

Aliko Dangote, the richest person in Africa, had humble beginnings. Born into a middle-class Nigerian family, Dangote made his first business transaction at the age of 21 with a loan from his uncle. Despite the volatile business environment in Nigeria and the challenges that came with running a business in the African market, Dangote turned a small trading company into a multibillion-dollar conglomerate, Dangote Group. His story showcases the importance of having a robust market understanding, vision, and resilience.

Cathy Hughes

Cathy Hughes, founder of Radio One (now Urban One), faced homelessness and countless rejections while trying to buy a radio station. As a single mother, she persevered and became the first African American woman to head a publicly traded company. Hughes's journey demonstrates how life skills such as perseverance, resilience, and determination, along with a passion for one's work, can overcome immense obstacles.

These additional narratives not only illustrate the power of perseverance, creativity, and resilience in the face of adversity but also underscore the impact of entrepreneurship as a tool for empowerment. These entrepreneurs saw challenges as opportunities, turned ideas into successful ventures, and in doing so, have paved the way for future generations.

These compelling narratives underline the value of entrepreneurial resilience, the application of 21st-century skills, and the significant impact that a single individual's success can have on broader societal and economic change. Their stories illuminate the path for future entrepreneurs and change-makers, demonstrating the power and potential of the Third Path.

Chapter 8: Removing Barriers to Entrepreneurship:

The Thinker and The Creator

Section 1: Identifying the Barriers

The journey to entrepreneurship, particularly for those who see themselves as thinkers and creators, is often fraught with both visible and invisible obstacles. Entrepreneurs, by their very nature, are innovative individuals who seek to create value in new and unique ways. However, their path is frequently hampered by systemic and societal barriers such as access to capital, availability of mentorship and networking opportunities, educational and skill disparities, racial and gender discrimination, and unfavorable regulatory conditions (Aldrich & Kim, 2007).

Access to capital is a significant hurdle, especially for underrepresented groups. Without the necessary funds, thinkers and creators may struggle to transform their innovative ideas into tangible businesses (Fairlie & Robb, 2008).

Mentorship and networking opportunities play a critical role in the entrepreneurial journey. They provide valuable advice, support, and connections that can help navigate the complex landscape of business, fostering a culture of shared knowledge and mutual growth (St-Jean & Audet, 2012). But these opportunities aren't evenly distributed, often making it challenging for those outside established networks to connect with mentors and peers.

The divide in education and skills can further complicate the entrepreneurial journey. It is not just about having a groundbreaking idea; entrepreneurs also need a broad range of skills—from business planning to marketing to financial management—to transform their ideas into successful enterprises (Edelman, Brush, & Manolova, 2008).

Additionally, racial and gender discrimination present subtle yet formidable challenges, especially for entrepreneurs from minority backgrounds. These entrepreneurs often encounter bias, making it even more challenging to secure funding, win customers, and build supportive communities (Fairlie & Robb, 2008).

Finally, regulatory conditions can make or break entrepreneurial ambitions. Overly complex or restrictive regulations can stifle creativity and innovation, especially for new and small businesses that may lack the resources to navigate these regulatory waters (Djankov, McLiesh, & Ramalho, 2006).

Reflection Question: Can you identify other potential barriers to entrepreneurship not discussed in this section? How do these barriers affect potential entrepreneurs, particularly thinkers and creators, in different contexts?

Understanding these barriers forms the basis for targeted interventions and policies that can help level the playing field for all entrepreneurs, enabling them to focus on what they do best: thinking creatively and creating value.

Section 2: Access to Capital and Resources

Capital is the lifeblood of any entrepreneurial endeavor, and it is here where many thinkers and creators, especially those from underrepresented backgrounds, encounter their first significant hurdle. Multiple studies indicate disparities in funding, with women and minority entrepreneurs consistently receiving less capital than their counterparts (Brush, Carter, Gatewood, Greene & Hart, 2001; Fairlie & Robb, 2008).

Often, these disparities can be traced back to institutional biases within the financial system. Traditional lending institutions have been critiqued for lending practices that unintentionally marginalize women and minority entrepreneurs (Cole, 2009). For creators and thinkers, the issue is compounded further. Their unconventional ideas might be overlooked by traditional lending systems that tend to favor proven business models over innovative yet risky propositions.

So, how can this funding gap be bridged? Crowdfunding presents a promising avenue. With the rise of platforms such as Kickstarter and Indiegogo, entrepreneurs now have the opportunity to present their ideas directly to the public. This democratizes access to capital and allows innovative thinkers and creators to secure funding based on the strength of their ideas rather than traditional credit evaluations (Mollick, 2014).

Microloans also serve as a viable solution. Organizations like Kiva and Grameen Bank offer small loans to entrepreneurs who might not qualify for traditional bank loans. These microloans can provide the initial capital needed for entrepreneurs to launch their ventures (Yunus, Moingeon, & Lehmann-Ortega, 2010).

Finally, venture capital funds specifically targeting underrepresented entrepreneurs have begun to emerge. By actively investing in diverse entrepreneurs, these funds not only provide much-needed capital but also contribute to building a more inclusive entrepreneurial ecosystem (Gompers & Wang, 2017).

Reflection Question: Can you think of other innovative ways to increase access to capital for underrepresented entrepreneurs?

While these solutions are promising, it's clear that access to capital remains a significant barrier for many entrepreneurs. By acknowledging and addressing these disparities, we can create a more equitable entrepreneurial landscape where thinkers and creators from all backgrounds have the opportunity to bring their ideas to life.

Section 3: Networks, Mentorship, and Education

Entrepreneurial success is not solely determined by financial resources. Equally vital are the benefits derived from social networks, mentorship, and entrepreneurial education (Hoang & Antoncic,

2003). Yet, access to these elements is often uneven, especially for Thinkers and Creators who may find themselves on the periphery of established networks and systems.

Social networks are crucial for gaining access to information, resources, and potential clients (Granovetter, 1983). But these networks are not easily accessible to everyone. For instance, aspiring entrepreneurs from underrepresented backgrounds often face challenges in infiltrating networks that have traditionally been homogeneous (Dale, 2004).

Reflection Question: How can we make professional networks more inclusive and accessible?

Mentorship is another area where disparities exist. Mentors can provide valuable advice, share experiences, and open doors to new opportunities (St-Jean & Audet, 2012). However, finding the right mentor can be particularly challenging for Thinkers and Creators, who often operate outside of traditional business spaces.

Think about this: How can we increase the availability of mentorship opportunities for Thinkers and Creators?

Entrepreneurial education is a vital component in preparing individuals for the challenges of entrepreneurship (Rae, 2010). Yet, traditional educational structures often neglect the needs of Thinkers and Creators. A focus on rote learning and standardized tests tends to undermine the cultivation of creative thinking, risk-taking, and innovation (Robinson, 2011).

Discussion Point: How can educational institutions better support the development of creative and innovative mindsets?

Fortunately, the digital age brings new opportunities to build networks, find mentors, and improve entrepreneurial education. Online platforms can facilitate connections across geographical and social boundaries, and educational initiatives can offer more tailored and flexible learning experiences. There's a need to leverage these tools to bridge the gap and foster a more inclusive entrepreneurial landscape.

Section 4: Policy and Regulatory Barriers

Entrepreneurs, particularly those who are Thinkers and Creators, often find themselves navigating intricate regulatory environments. While some regulation is necessary to maintain ethical and standard practices, an overly restrictive regulatory framework can stifle growth and innovation (Djankov et al., 2002).

Take, for instance, the process of business registration. In some regions, the bureaucracy involved in starting a business is time-consuming and complex, creating an unnecessary hurdle for potential entrepreneurs (Klapper et al., 2006).

Question for Reflection: How might bureaucratic procedures pose a challenge to new businesses?

Moreover, regulations around taxes, licensing, and permits can vary widely and change frequently, making it difficult for small businesses to stay compliant (Guzman & Stern, 2015). This is particularly challenging for Thinkers and Creators who often lack the resources to hire legal or financial consultants.

Discussion Point: How can regulatory clarity and consistency be ensured for small businesses?

Lastly, sector-specific regulations can also pose barriers. For example, the tech industry, where many Thinkers and Creators operate, is often subject to intense scrutiny and rapidly evolving rules around data protection, privacy, and intellectual property (Aldrich, 2012).

Think about this: How can policy better support innovation in highly regulated sectors?

Potential policy changes that could foster a more entrepreneur-friendly environment include simplifying business registration processes, offering clear and consistent regulatory guidelines, and ensuring policies reflect the needs and realities of different sectors. Policymakers and stakeholders need to collaborate to create a regulatory environment that not only protects the public interest but also promotes entrepreneurial activity.

Section 5: Overcoming Discrimination

Discrimination remains a profound challenge for many entrepreneurs, especially those who identify as Thinkers and Creators. These individuals often view the world through a unique lens and approach problems differently, which can lead to them being misunderstood or marginalized (Aldrich & Kim, 2007).

Question for Reflection: How can the unique perspective of a Thinker or Creator become a barrier in a traditional business environment?

Discrimination can take many forms, including racial, gender, or age bias, and can have a significant impact on entrepreneurial activity. For instance, research shows that women and minority entrepreneurs often struggle to secure funding compared to their white male counterparts (Robb & Fairlie, 2007). Additionally, these entrepreneurs might lack role models and mentors, face harsher scrutiny, and have fewer opportunities to network and forge business relationships (Fairlie & Robb, 2008).

Discussion Point: How does discrimination create unequal opportunities for different groups of entrepreneurs?

Thankfully, many organizations and initiatives are committed to fostering diversity and inclusion within the entrepreneurial ecosystem. This can involve developing programs that specifically target underrepresented entrepreneurs, providing them with mentorship, resources, and networking opportunities (Brush et al., 2018).

Additionally, implementing unconscious bias training can help investors, stakeholders, and fellow entrepreneurs understand and overcome their biases, leading to a more inclusive and equitable entrepreneurial environment (Devine et al., 2012).

Think about this: How can we effectively address unconscious bias within the entrepreneurial ecosystem?

Ultimately, overcoming discrimination requires a concerted effort from all involved in the entrepreneurial journey - from the entrepreneurs themselves to investors, policymakers, and society at large. By acknowledging and actively addressing these biases, we can pave the way for a more inclusive, diverse, and successful entrepreneurial landscape.

Case Study : Julia Collins, Planet FWD and Zume Pizza

Julia Collins, co-founder of Zume Pizza and founder of Planet FWD, is another testament to the power of tenacity and vision in overcoming entrepreneurial barriers (Denham, 2020). As a Black woman in the tech industry, Collins had to navigate both racial and gender biases.

Reflection Question: How can being a woman and a racial minority compound the challenges faced by entrepreneurs?

Despite these challenges, Collins successfully raised venture capital for both her startups, breaking barriers as one of the few Black women to have co-founded a unicorn company (Burt, 2021). She credits her success to a combination of her unique perspective, commitment to her vision, and the building of a supportive network.

Discussion Point: How does a unique perspective serve as an asset in entrepreneurship?

By examining the stories of successful entrepreneurs like Walker and Collins, we gain valuable insights into how barriers can be overcome. Their journeys highlight the importance of perseverance, vision, networking, access to resources, and the ability to leverage one's unique perspective as key factors in surmounting the challenges faced by entrepreneurs.

"Section 6: Looking Ahead: Creating an Inclusive Entrepreneurial Ecosystem

As we envision a future where the entrepreneurial ecosystem is inclusive and empowering for all, we must remember the wisdom of Booker T. Washington and W.E.B. Du Bois. Both leaders recognized the importance of education, hard work, and empowerment, though their approaches differed. As we chart a way forward, we see that both of these paths are crucial to entrepreneurial success, forming a 'Third Path' that combines the practical skills and self-reliance espoused by Washington with Du Bois' advocacy for civil rights, higher education, and political representation.

On an individual level, fostering an entrepreneurial mindset—much like Washington's emphasis on self-reliance—is crucial. It entails developing resilience, creativity, and a willingness to take calculated risks, as well as actively seeking educational opportunities, mentorship, and networking events to gain the necessary skills and connections. This pursuit of knowledge and skills aligns with Du Bois' call for higher education.

Question for Reflection: How can you incorporate the philosophies of Washington and Du Bois in your entrepreneurial journey?

At the community level, initiatives like local entrepreneurship workshops, mentorship programs, and networking events can create a supportive environment, similar to Washington's vision of community upliftment. Local businesses and successful entrepreneurs can also offer resources, share knowledge, and create opportunities for underrepresented entrepreneurs—echoing Du Bois' call for empowerment through representation.

Reflect on this: How can your community foster an entrepreneurial environment that encapsulates the philosophies of Washington and Du Bois?

At the societal level, just as Du Bois championed civil rights, we must advocate for changes in policy and regulation that create a more inclusive entrepreneurial ecosystem. Policies promoting access to capital for underrepresented entrepreneurs, and regulations encouraging diversity and inclusion in business can have a significant impact.

Question for Reflection: What societal changes do you believe are necessary to create an inclusive entrepreneurial ecosystem that honors the visions of both Washington and Du Bois?

By integrating the philosophies of Washington and Du Bois into modern entrepreneurial thinking, we can create a 'Third Path'—an approach that empowers individuals to realize their entrepreneurial ambitions, regardless of their background. This path encourages the development of practical skills for immediate benefit while also advocating for systemic change for long-term progress, thus merging the philosophies of these great thinkers into a unified vision for the future.

Chapter 9: Education for a New Era:

Instilling Entrepreneurial Thinking

Section 1: The Role of Education in Fostering Entrepreneurship

Educational systems play a critical role in cultivating entrepreneurial skills and mindset. Booker T. Washington, an advocate for practical skills and self-reliance, once said, "In all things social we can be as separate as the fingers, yet one as the hand in all things essential to mutual progress" (Washington, 1903). His ideas underscore the need for a holistic approach to education—one that integrates various skills to prepare students for real-world challenges.

The advent of STEM (Science, Technology, Engineering, and Math) and STEAM (Science, Technology, Engineering, Arts, and Math) in schools is a significant step toward this goal. These programs emphasize problem-solving, critical thinking, and creativity —essential entrepreneurial skills (Honey, Pearson & Schweingruber, 2014). Georgia has also started offering entrepreneurship as a vocational option in the CTAE (Career, Technical, and Agricultural

Education) pathway. However, these initiatives, while promising, are only the beginning.

We need to delve deeper into how these entrepreneurial skills can be incorporated more broadly into the curriculum. Creativity, a key driver of innovation and entrepreneurial thinking, can be nurtured in schools through hands-on projects that encourage students to design solutions to real-world problems (Resnick, 2017).

Critical thinking and problem-solving echo W.E.B. Du Bois's emphasis on higher education and can be fostered by incorporating complex, open-ended problems into the curriculum instead of focusing solely on rote learning (Paul & Elder, 2006). Du Bois asserted, "Of all the civil rights for which the world has struggled and fought for 5,000 years, the right to learn is undoubtedly the most fundamental..." (Du Bois, 1949). This encourages students to question, evaluate, and make decisions, preparing them for the dynamic and uncertain landscape of entrepreneurship.

Resilience, a trait that allows entrepreneurs to persist despite challenges, aligns with both Washington's and Du Bois' philosophies of perseverance in the face of adversity. This can be cultivated by providing supportive environments where mistakes are considered learning opportunities (Reivich & Shatté, 2002).

In conclusion, the pathway toward an educational system that nurtures entrepreneurial skills requires more than introducing new subjects or pathways. It calls for a fundamental shift in how we view and implement education—a blend of the practical and the intellectual, inspired by the philosophies of Washington and Du Bois.

Let's dive deeper into how Finland and Singapore successfully implemented entrepreneurial thinking in their education systems:

Case Study 1: Finland's Progressive Approach

Finland's education system is characterized by its student-centered approach, where the focus is on developing critical and creative thinking skills from an early age. The country has integrated entrepreneurship education as a cross-curricular theme throughout the schooling years, from primary education to upper secondary education.

The approach is not about directly teaching entrepreneurship as a subject but rather fostering entrepreneurial attitudes and skills. This is achieved through pedagogical practices that emphasize problem-solving, innovation, and active learning. For instance, students might be tasked with running mini-businesses, managing classroom resources, or creating solutions for community problems. The success of this approach is reflected in the high levels of student engagement, creativity, and motivation (Finnish National Agency for Education, 2020).

Case Study 2: Singapore's Structured Approach

Singapore has adopted a more structured approach to inculcating an entrepreneurial mindset. The Ministry of Education has introduced numerous initiatives, such as the Applied Learning Programmes (ALPs) and Innovation Programmes. The ALPs expose students to experiential learning through real-world scenarios, while the Innovation Programmes aim to nurture a spirit of innovation and entrepreneurship.

At the higher education level, institutions like the National University of Singapore have established dedicated entrepreneurship centers. These centers provide students with mentorship, funding, and resources to start their ventures. The success of these initiatives can be seen in the rising number of student-led start-ups and the increased interest in entrepreneurship among Singapore's youth (Ministry of Education, Singapore, 2019).

In essence, both Finland and Singapore have taken significant steps towards integrating entrepreneurial thinking into their educational systems. While their approaches differ, both have had substantial success, emphasizing that there's more than one way to instill an entrepreneurial mindset in students.

Reflection Question: Considering the depth of Finland's and Singapore's integration of entrepreneurial thinking into their education, what elements could potentially be implemented in your local education system?

Section 3: Challenges and Opportunities

Implementing entrepreneurial thinking into educational curricula presents several challenges. One of the major obstacles is the rigid structure of most traditional education systems that are geared towards standardization and rote learning, leaving little room for creative thinking and problem-solving (Robinson, 2011).

Another challenge lies in the training of educators. To effectively teach entrepreneurial skills, teachers need to be trained in fostering creativity, innovation, and problem-solving. However, many educators may not have received this type of training (Fretschner & Weber, 2013).

Despite these challenges, incorporating entrepreneurial thinking into education brings tremendous opportunities. It allows students to develop a growth mindset, become self-directed learners, and be better prepared for the uncertainties and complexities of the 21st-century workplace (Dweck, 2006). It also fosters a culture of innovation and resilience that can drive societal growth and development (Mwasalwiba, 2010).

To overcome these challenges, a systematic approach is needed. This could involve rethinking educational policies to allow more flexibility, offering professional development programs for educators, and forging partnerships with industry to ensure the relevance of what is taught in the classroom.

Reflection Question: Reflecting on these challenges and opportunities, how can your community or institution foster entrepreneurial thinking within the current educational landscape? What specific actions can you take?

Section 4: Looking Ahead: Strategies for Implementing Entrepreneurial Education

Implementing entrepreneurial education requires a concerted effort from educators, policymakers, and community leaders. Here are some strategies for doing so:

1. Revamp Curriculum: Incorporate elements of entrepreneurial thinking, such as creativity, problem-solving, and risk-taking, into the curriculum across all subjects (Volkmann et al., 2009). This can be done through project-based learning, experiential learning activities, and incorporating real-world examples and case studies.
2. Train Teachers: Provide professional development for teachers to equip them with the skills and knowledge to foster entrepreneurial thinking in students (Heinonen & Poikkijoki, 2006).
3. Foster a Supportive Environment: Create an environment that encourages creativity, experimentation, and failure. This includes setting up spaces for innovation in schools, such as makerspaces or innovation labs, and adopting grading policies that reward creativity and innovation (Cannon & Edmondson, 2005).
4. Build Community Partnerships: Partner with local businesses, nonprofits, and other organizations to provide students with real-world entrepreneurial experiences. This could include internships, mentorship programs, and community projects.

Reflection Question: Based on these strategies, what steps can you take in your own context to foster entrepreneurial education? How can you leverage the resources in your community to provide real-world entrepreneurial experiences for students?

Chapter 10: Policy Proposals for a Nation of Creators

Section 1: Shaping Policies for an Entrepreneurial Future

In an increasingly complex and interconnected world, fostering an entrepreneurial mindset is critical for innovation, economic growth, and social development. Policy plays a pivotal role in shaping this entrepreneurial future. It sets the parameters within which individuals and businesses operate, providing a framework that can either encourage or stifle entrepreneurial activity.

Different policy areas play unique roles in this context. Education policy, for instance, has the potential to instill entrepreneurial thinking right from the early years, molding creative and critical thinkers who can spot opportunities and drive change. Policies related to economic development can stimulate entrepreneurial activity by creating an environment conducive to business creation and growth. This can include policies to enhance access to finance, build supportive infrastructure, and create a favorable business regulatory environment.

Regulation policy, too, has a significant role. While regulation is essential to maintain fair competition and protect public interest, overly restrictive or complicated regulations can impede entrepreneurial activity. Therefore, a balanced approach that protects the public interest without stifling innovation is crucial.

Finally, innovation policy is key to creating a nation of creators. Policies that support research and development, protect intellectual property rights, and stimulate collaboration between universities and businesses can drive innovation and entrepreneurship.

An interdisciplinary and collaborative approach in policy-making is crucial to align these different areas. This requires breaking down silos, encouraging dialogue and cooperation between different policy areas, and promoting a shared vision of an entrepreneurial future.

Reflection Question: In considering policy as a tool to foster an entrepreneurial mindset and create a nation of creators, which policy area do you believe holds the greatest potential and why? What specific changes in this area would you propose to nurture an entrepreneurial society?

Specific policy changes could include the incorporation of entrepreneurship education at all levels, from elementary school to higher education. Entrepreneurship education, as argued by Fayolle and Gailly (2015), not only equips students with skills to start a business but also fosters creativity, resilience, and adaptability.

To truly foster an entrepreneurial future, we need to address the challenges faced by thinkers and creators of the past like W.E.B Du Bois and Booker T. Washington, and the barriers that persist today.

In the early 20th century, both Du Bois and Washington advocated for African American education, albeit with different approaches. Washington, founder of Tuskegee Institute, believed in industrial education, arguing that learning practical skills would provide immediate economic benefits and improve the social status of African Americans. Du Bois, on the other hand, emphasized a "classical" education that encouraged intellectual growth and the development of leadership skills to challenge racial discrimination.

Their differing perspectives underscore a key barrier that remains relevant today: striking a balance between practical skills and intellectual growth. Policy needs to ensure that education promotes both these aspects to foster entrepreneurial thinking.

Another challenge that both Du Bois and Washington encountered was racial discrimination, which limited the opportunities available to African Americans. Today, discrimination continues to hinder the progress of marginalized communities, including in entrepreneurship. Therefore, anti-discrimination laws and diversity initiatives must be a part of any policy efforts to foster entrepreneurship.

Policymakers, educators, and society at large coming together to realize this vision of an entrepreneurial future necessitates a multifaceted approach.

Policymakers have the power to shape the regulatory and financial landscape. They can provide incentives for schools and educators to integrate entrepreneurial thinking into their curriculums, and make it a priority in policy plans. For instance, providing additional funding to schools that incorporate entrepreneurial learning or offering tax benefits to companies that invest in educational initiatives can incentivize the shift towards a more entrepreneurial education system.

Educators, on the other hand, have the crucial task of implementation. They can experiment with innovative pedagogical techniques that foster creativity and entrepreneurial skills, and contribute their experiences and learnings to broader policy discussions. Professional development programs can equip educators with the necessary skills and knowledge to teach entrepreneurship effectively.

Current barriers that need policy intervention include access to resources and capital, quality education, and regulatory challenges. As previously discussed, policymakers can provide incentives to encourage entrepreneurial learning and alleviate financial barriers. They can also create a regulatory environment that is supportive of new ventures.

By recognizing the challenges faced by pioneering thinkers and creators like Du Bois and Washington and addressing current barriers, we can shape policies that truly support an entrepreneurial future.

Reflection Question: How can lessons from the past inform policy changes to foster entrepreneurship?

Society at large plays an essential role. Parents and communities can advocate for these educational changes and provide additional support to students as they develop entrepreneurial skills. Businesses and community organizations can partner with schools to offer real-world experiences and mentorship to students.

However, to ensure that these changes are implemented effectively, it is critical to establish systems for monitoring and evaluation. Collecting data on student outcomes and periodically reviewing the effectiveness of the changes can provide valuable feedback and enable continual improvement.

In short, transforming education to foster an entrepreneurial mindset is a collective responsibility. It requires the concerted effort of all stakeholders, from policymakers to educators, from parents to community organizations, and the students themselves. Only then can we build an education system that truly empowers students to become creators and entrepreneurs.

Section 2: Fostering Innovation Through Policy

Innovation, the heartbeat of entrepreneurial ventures, requires a conducive policy environment to thrive. Policymakers have several tools at their disposal to stimulate and protect innovation.

One such tool is intellectual property (IP) law, which plays a vital role in promoting innovation by protecting the rights of inventors. Through patents, copyrights, and trademarks, creators can safeguard their inventions from being used without their permission, incentivizing further innovation. For instance, the United States Patent and Trademark Office grants patents to inventors, securing their exclusive rights and fostering an environment of innovation (USPTO, 2021).

Research and Development (R&D) funding is another significant policy area. Public funding for research can lead to groundbreaking innovations that might be too risky or long-term for private companies to undertake. For instance, the internet, GPS, and touchscreen technology were all born out of publicly funded research. Governments can also provide tax incentives to private companies to encourage them to invest more in R&D.

Finally, policymakers can foster innovation through the creation of innovation clusters. These are geographic concentrations of interconnected companies and institutions in a particular field. Silicon Valley is perhaps the most famous example of such a cluster. Policies that encourage the development of such clusters can lead to increased innovation, as the close proximity of various stakeholders leads to the exchange of ideas and collaboration.

Discussion Point: Policies related to intellectual property rights, research and development funding, and the creation of innovation clusters can greatly foster innovation. How can these policy areas be optimized to further encourage creativity and entrepreneurial thinking?

Section 3: Case Studies: Policy Initiatives Supporting Entrepreneurship

This part will highlight policy initiatives across the globe that have positively impacted the entrepreneurial ecosystem. By exploring these successful endeavors, we can glean insights into how different regions navigate the complex nexus of entrepreneurship and policy.

Case Study 1: Singapore's Startup Ecosystem

Singapore has strategically transformed itself into a global startup hub. Its government realized the potential of technology-based startups early on and established the Technology Incubation Scheme (TIS) under the Agency for Science, Technology, and Research (ASTAR) in 2011. *The TIS offers start-ups venture co-funding, where the government provides 85% of the investment (up to SGD 500,000), encouraging venture capitalists to invest in technology-based startups (ASTAR, 2022).* This policy has mitigated the initial financial risks for both investors and startups, resulting in a thriving tech startup ecosystem that contributes to the country's economic growth and innovation.

Case Study 2: Germany's Mittelstand

The backbone of the German economy, the Mittelstand, refers to a unique cluster of small and medium-sized enterprises (SMEs). This sector traces back to Germany's historical craftsmanship traditions and has been consciously preserved and nurtured through targeted government policies. These firms receive tax breaks, research funding, and special consideration in public procurement. Through these policies, the German government has helped create a resilient economy that emphasizes long-term growth over short-term profit, supporting community stability, providing employment, and driving innovation.

Case Study 3: Chile's Start-Up Chile program

Launched in 2010 by the Chilean Government, Start-Up Chile was designed to transform the nation into the innovation and entrepreneurial hub of Latin America. The program offers selected startups equity-free investment, one-year working visas, and a plethora of training and networking opportunities. By attracting international startups, Chile has diversified its economy, spurred job creation, and invigorated its entrepreneurial scene.

Each of these case studies serves as a testament to the role of supportive policy frameworks in fostering entrepreneurship. They highlight how concerted and well-thought-out policy measures can bolster entrepreneurship, bringing socio-economic benefits to a nation.

Section 4: Looking Ahead: Crafting Policy for a Nation of Creators

As we consider a future where entrepreneurship and creativity form the basis of our national identity, policy will play an integral role. It is essential to design and implement strategies that not only support, but actively encourage and develop a nation of creators.

Drawing from the legacy of W.E.B. DuBois and Booker T. Washington, we see that while their methods and immediate objectives differed, they shared a common goal: the upliftment and progress of African Americans through education and economic development. DuBois advocated for higher education as a means to develop the "Talented Tenth", the leaders who would uplift their communities. Washington, on the other hand, emphasized practical, vocational training and entrepreneurship as a path to economic independence and respect

.

As we craft policy for a nation of creators, it's necessary to weave together these distinct, yet interconnected strands. To do so, three key strategies can be proposed:

1. Interdisciplinary Education: Policymakers should strive for an educational framework that fosters entrepreneurial thinking, drawing on DuBois's advocacy for intellectual development, and Washington's emphasis on practical skills.
2. Support for Entrepreneurs: Government policies should provide support and incentives for individuals, especially from disadvantaged backgrounds, to pursue entrepreneurial ventures.
3. Stakeholder Involvement: Policies should be designed with the active participation of educators, entrepreneurs, and community leaders to ensure they are responsive and well-targeted.

Reflecting on these strategies, it becomes clear that policy development is an ongoing process that must remain adaptive to the evolving needs of society.

Reflection Question: How can we ensure that our policies keep pace with the evolving landscape of entrepreneurship and creativity? What mechanisms can be put in place to allow for the ongoing evaluation and adaptation of these policies?

Conclusion: Toward a Future of Thinkers and Creators

As we close this exploration into a Third Path, it becomes clear that the lessons drawn from both W.E.B. DuBois and Booker T. Washington's philosophies have critical relevance today. Their differing yet complementary visions—one emphasizing the intellectual power of higher education, the other highlighting the pragmatic strength of entrepreneurial skills and economic independence—have the potential to guide us towards a future where everyone, regardless of color or economic status, can contribute to building thriving communities and a flourishing nation.

The Third Path, an amalgamation of these visions, proposes an empowered society of thinkers and creators, individuals who possess the ability and the initiative to shape their own destinies, to drive innovation, and to spur economic growth. This is a dramatic shift from the assembly-line workers that industrialists like John D. Rockefeller once envisioned as the backbone of the economy. The Third Path goes beyond color, beyond economic status, embracing the individual strengths and talents that make us unique, cultivating a nation where all ideas are respected, and creativity thrives.

If you have journeyed with us through this book, we hope you are inspired. Inspired to see the potential within yourself and within every individual you encounter. Inspired to foster this potential, not only in your local community but globally. Inspired to change the world through innovation and love, in a way that aligns with our shared human aspiration for peace and harmony.

This is not an easy task, nor is it a swift one. It requires commitment, courage, and above all, belief. Belief in the potential within every individual to create and contribute. The problem is not elsewhere, the solution is within us. The next Mark Zuckerberg, Jeff Bezos, Elon Musk, or Sam Walton could be anywhere—a small village in Africa, a bustling city in Asia, a serene town in Europe, or a vibrant neighborhood in America. They could be anywhere, in anyone

.

In the words of Mahatma Gandhi, "You must be the change you wish to see in the world". This call to action is as relevant today as ever. As we look toward the future, let us strive to foster an environment that empowers individuals to become thinkers and creators, fostering a world teeming with innovation and driven by the powerful engine of human potential.

As you close this book, consider this question: How will you contribute to this vision of a world of thinkers and creators? What steps will you take today to help cultivate a nation of independent creators?

Let's change the world together.

Glossary

Access to Capital: The ability for an individual or business to obtain funds as financing, investment, or credit.

Bricolage: Making creative and resourceful use of whatever materials are at hand (regardless of their original purpose).

Booker T. Washington: An influential African American leader who believed in practical education and entrepreneurship as means for African Americans to achieve economic independence.

Capitalism: An economic and political system in which a country's trade and industry are controlled by private owners for profit, rather than by the state.

Collective Impact: A commitment of a group of important actors from different sectors to a common agenda for solving a specific social problem.

Critical Thinking: The objective analysis and evaluation of an issue to form a judgement.

Digital Divide: The gap between those who have ready access to computers and the internet, and those who do not.

Digital Literacy: The ability to use information and communication technologies to find, evaluate, create, and communicate information.

Disruptive Technology: New technology that disrupts the status quo, displacing an established technology and shaking up the industry.

Du Boisian Philosophy of Education: A philosophy that stresses the importance of intellectual education for African Americans in addition to industrial training, named after W.E.B. Du Bois.

Economic Equity: A state in which individuals, irrespective of their demographic identity, have fair access to economic resources and opportunities such as capital, education, and employment.

Entrepreneurial Mindset: A set of attitudes, skills and behaviors that individuals can use to create value in their lives and the lives of others.

Entrepreneurship: The process of starting, developing, and managing a business venture in order to gain profit by taking several risks in the corporate world.

Gig Economy: A labor market characterized by the prevalence of short-term contracts or freelance work as opposed to permanent jobs.

Incubator: An organization that helps develop early-stage companies, often providing workspace, mentoring, education, and access to funding.

Inclusive Innovation: An approach that aims to improve the opportunities for all individuals, particularly those who are underserved or marginalized, to participate in and benefit from the innovation process.

Innovation: The process of translating an idea or invention into a good or service that creates value for which customers will pay.

Makerspace: A collaborative workspace inside a school, library, or public/private facility for making, learning, exploring and sharing.

Microloan: A small loan, typically in the range of a few hundred to several thousand dollars, issued to small business owners or aspiring entrepreneurs.

Nascent Entrepreneur: An individual in the process of establishing a business venture.

Patent: A government authority or license conferring a right or title for a set period, especially the sole right to exclude others from making, using, or selling an invention.

Public-Private Partnership: A cooperative arrangement between two or more public and private sectors, typically of a long-term nature.

Resilience: The ability to recover quickly from difficulties; toughness.

Social Capital: The networks of relationships among people who live and work in a particular society, enabling that society to function effectively.

Social Entrepreneurship: The use of start-up companies and other entrepreneurs to develop, fund and implement solutions to social, cultural, or environmental issues.

Soft Skills: Personal attributes that enable someone to interact effectively and harmoniously with other people.

Start-up: A newly established business.

STEM Education: An interdisciplinary approach to learning where academic concepts are coupled with real-world situations.

Sustainable Development: Development that meets the needs of the present without compromising the ability of future generations to meet their own needs.

About The Author

Dr. Anton Anthony, Ed. S, ThD has served in school districts throughout Georgia as a teacher, discipline coordinator, coach, assistant principal, and principal.

He has worked in poverty-stricken schools where most of the population was Title I. He has also worked in schools where parents were highly educated, high-income professionals and business owners. Each school brought its own challenges, but he was able to break through barriers and achieve academic improvement everywhere he went.

Credentials

Dr. Anthony received his Bachelor of Arts with Honors in Business Management from Fort Valley State University in Georgia. He received his Masters of Arts in Teaching at Augusta State University. He later returned to receive a degree in Curriculum and Instruction from Augusta University and received his Educational Specialist add-on in Educational Leadership and Administration, also at Augusta University. He holds his Doctorate in Theology from North Central Theological Seminary. He is a licensed educator and real estate broker with the State of Georgia.

Career

He began his educational career as a reading specialist in Burke County, Georgia schools. He was moved into the 7th grade English/Language Arts program (ELA), where he experienced his first real taste of educational success. His class achieved the highest passing percentage, and he was given an award to recognize his achievement.

After spending a second year at the middle school where he began his career, he asked for a position as a coach at an alternative school in that same district. Former teacher of the year for the school, he was allowed to become the coach, discipline coordinator, and reading instructor.

From those positions, he would become an assistant principal and principal. He is currently a public school principal in Georgia to be closer to his children.

Current Status

Mr. Anthony currently lives in Georgia. He is one of the most active administrators on social media and looks forward to bringing his vision of AA STEAM & Entrepreneurship Academy to life.

References

1. Alperovitz, G., Dubb, S., & Howard, T. (2009). The Cleveland Model. The Nation.
2. Anderson, J. D. (1988). The Education of Blacks in the South, 1860-1935. University of North Carolina Press.
3. Anderson, M. (2021). 7% of Americans don't use the internet. Who are they?. Pew Research Center.
4. A*STAR. (2022). Technology Incubation Scheme. Retrieved from https://www.a-star.edu.sg
5. Audretsch, D. B., & Keilbach, M. (2004). Entrepreneurship and regional growth: An evolutionary interpretation. Journal of Evolutionary Economics.
6. Belitski, M., & Desai, S. (2016). Creativity, education and entrepreneurship. Journal of Technology Transfer.
7. Brynjolfsson, E., & McAfee, A. (2014). The Second Machine Age: Work, Progress, and Prosperity in a Time of Brilliant Technologies. W. W. Norton & Company.
8. Carnegie, A. (1889). The Gospel of Wealth. North American Review.
9. Cannon, M. D., & Edmondson, A. C. (2005). Failing to learn and learning to fail (intelligently): How great organizations put failure to work to innovate and improve. Long range planning, 38(3), 299-319.
10. Centers for Disease Control and Prevention. (2021). COVID-19 Racial and Ethnic Health Disparities.
11. Chui, M., Manyika, J., Miremadi, M. (2020). Where machines could replace humans—and where they can't (yet). Brookings Institution.

12. Desa, G. (2012). Resource Mobilization in International Social Entrepreneurship: Bricolage as a Mechanism of Institutional Transformation. Entrepreneurship Theory and Practice, 36(4), 727–751.
13. Du Bois, W. E. B. (1903). The Souls of Black Folk. A.C. McClurg & Co.
14. Du Bois, W. E. B. (1903). The Talented Tenth. In The Negro Problem: A Series of Articles by Representative American Negroes of To-Day. New York: James Pott & Co.
15. Du Bois, W. E. B. (1949). The Right to Learn. The Phi Delta Kappan, 31(6), 241-244.
16. Dweck, C. (2006). Mindset: The new psychology of success. Random House.
17. Eesley, D. E., & Longenecker, C. O. (2006). Gateways to entrepreneurship: An innovative program introduces students to the world of small business. International Journal of Management Education.
18. Edelman, L. F., Manolova, T., & Brush, C. (2008). Entrepreneurship education: Correspondence between practices of nascent entrepreneurs and textbook prescriptions for success. Academy of Management Learning & Education.
19. Fairlie, R. (2020). The Impact of COVID-19 on Small Business Owners: Evidence of Early-Stage Losses from the April 2020 Current Population Survey. University of California Santa Cruz.
20. Fairlie, R. W. (2013). Entrepreneurship, economic conditions, and the Great Recession. Journal of Economics & Management Strategy, 22(2), 207-231.
21. Finnish National Agency for Education. (2020). Entrepreneurship education in Finland. Finnish National Agency for Education.
22. Frame, W. S., Wall, L. D., & White, L. J. (2002). The Disruptive Influence of Technology on Competition in Retail Banking. Federal Reserve Bank of Atlanta.
23. Fretschner, M., & Weber, S. (2013). Measuring and understanding the effects of entrepreneurial awareness education. Journal of Small Business Management.
24. Haltiwanger, J., Jarmin, R. S., & Miranda, J. (2013). Who creates jobs? Small vs. large vs. young. The Review of Economics and Statistics, 95(2), 347-361.
25. Harlan, L. R. (1983). Booker T. Washington: The Making of a Black Leader, 1856-1901. Oxford University Press.

26. Heinonen, J., & Poikkijoki, S. A. (2006). An entrepreneurial-directed approach to entrepreneurship education: mission impossible?. Journal of Management Development.
27. Holzer, H. J. (1996). What Employers Want: Job Prospects for Less-Educated Workers. Russell Sage Foundation.
28. Honey, M., Pearson, G., & Schweingruber, A. (2014). STEM Integration in K-12 Education: Status, Prospects, and an Agenda for Research. National Academies Press.
29. Kantor, H., & Lowe, R. (2006). From New Deal to No Deal: No Child Left Behind and the Devolution of Responsibility for Equal Opportunity. Harvard Educational Review, 76(4), 474-502.
30. Krueger, N. F., & Brazeal, D. V. (1994). Entrepreneurial potential and potential entrepreneurs. Entrepreneurship Theory and Practice.
31. Mazzucato, M. (2013). The Entrepreneurial State: Debunking Public vs. Private Sector Myths. London: Anthem Press.
32. Ministry of Education, Singapore. (2019). Nurturing students for the future - Innovations for teaching and learning. Ministry of Education, Singapore.
33. Mwasalwiba, E. S. (2010). Entrepreneurship education: a review of its objectives, teaching methods, and impact indicators. Education + Training.
34. Mutlu, B., Er, E., Kocadere, S.A. (2018). The Effect of Project-Based Learning on the Creative Thinking Skills of Entrepreneurial Learning Students. Thinking Skills and Creativity, 28, 38-48.
35. OECD. (2022). Entrepreneurship at a Glance. Retrieved from https://www.oecd.org
36. Paul, R., & Elder, L. (2006). Critical thinking: The nature of critical and creative thought. Journal of Developmental Education, 30(2), 34.
37. Porter, M. E. (1998). Clusters and the new economics of competition. Harvard Business Review, 76(6), 77-90.
38. Reivich, K., & Shatté, A. (2002). The Resilience Factor: 7 Essential Skills for Overcoming Life's Inevitable Obstacles. Broadway Books.
39. Resnick, M. (2017). Lifelong kindergarten: Cultivating creativity through projects, passion, peers, and play. MIT Press.
40. Robinson, K. (2011). Out of our minds: Learning to be creative. Capstone Publishing Ltd.
41. Rockfeller, J. D. (1909). The Difficult Art of Giving. The World's Work, 18, 12166–12174.
42. Saxenian, A. (1994). Regional Advantage: Culture and Competition in Silicon Valley and Route 128. Harvard University Press.

43. Start-Up Chile. (2022). About Us. Retrieved from https://www.startupchile.org
44. Suri, T., & Jack, W. (2016). The long-run poverty and gender impacts of mobile money. Science, 354(6317), 1288-1292.
45. Taylor JR, Lovell ST (2015) Urban home food gardens in the Global North: research traditions and future directions. Agric Hum Values.
46. Ulukaya, H. (2019). The Anti-CEO Playbook. TED Talk.
47. USPTO. (2021). Patent Process Overview. Retrieved from https://www.uspto.gov/patents/basics
48. U.S. Small Business Administration. (2012). Frequently Asked Questions.
49. Vance, A. (2015). Elon Musk: Tesla, SpaceX, and the Quest for a Fantastic Future. HarperCollins.
50. Volkmann, C., Wilson, K. E., Mariotti, S., Rabuzzi, D., Vyakarnam, S., & Sepulveda, A. (2009). Educating the next wave of entrepreneurs: unlocking entrepreneurial capabilities to meet the global challenges.
51. Washington, B. T. (1903). Up from Slavery: An Autobiography. Doubleday, Page & Co.
52. Welter, F. (2011). Contextualizing Entrepreneurship—Conceptual Challenges and Ways Forward. Entrepreneurship Theory and Practice.
53. Yunus, M., & Weber, K. (2007). Creating a World Without Poverty: Social Business and the Future of Capitalism. PublicAffairs.

Connect With The Author

Contact Information

To connect with Mr. Anthony online, you can find him online.
Facebook: http://facebook.com/anton.anthony1

Twitter:

https://Twitter.com/antonanthony5

Instagram:

Instagram.com/authorantonanthony

LinkedIn:

www.linkedin.com/in/authorantonanthonysr

YouTube:

https://www.youtube.com/channel/UCI77nqy8OXItxQ_Zaz-NSm0w

Email:

AAStemAcademy@gmail.com

antonanthonysr@gmail.com

contact@authorantonanthony.com

www.ingramcontent.com/pod-product-compliance
Lightning Source LLC
Chambersburg PA
CBHW050438010526

44118CB00013B/1588